WELCOME

Get ready to rewind the cassette and crank up the nostalgia – here's your backstage pass to the wonderful world of 90s boybands! From frosted tips to synchronised dance moves, we're diving into the era when harmonies and dramatic key changes ruled the charts and posters covered every teen's bedroom wall. Whether you swooned over Take That or spent your Saturdays learning the latest dance moves to NSYNC's hits with pals, this is your ultimate guide to the heartthrobs, hits and hysteria that made the 90s totally unforgettable!

 WARNING: PULSE-RAISING POP PERFECTION INSIDE!

CONTENTS

6 THE EARLY YEARS

- 8 **Ultimate Take That:** Part 1
- 12 **Real Life:** A Million Love Songs By Special Delivery
- 14 Ultimate East 17
- 18 Ultimate Boyzone
- 22 **Pin-up:** NSYNC
- 24 Best 90s Boyband Videos
- 26 **Real Life:** Behind The Scenes Of Shout
- 54 **Real Life:** Star Maker
- 56 Guess The Lyric!

30 VINTAGE SHOUT MAGAZINE

- 32 Take That Go Mad in Paris
- 34 I'm Obsessed with Take That
- 36 Bad Boys Inc Kiss And Tell
- 38 Battle Of The Bands
- 41 Boytalk with Boyzone and Atlantic 252
- 42 Five On Fame
- 44 Boyzone Behind The Scenes
- 46 Boytalk with Backstreet Boys
- 48 **Pin-up:** 911 plus interview
- 51 **Facts:** East 17
- 52 Boyband Gossip

58 MID-LATE 1990s

- 60 Ultimate Take That: Part 2
- 64 Did You Know?
- 66 Ultimate 911
- 68 **Real Life:** Ronan Who?
- 70 Ultimate Five
- 74 **Real Life:** Pure Bliss
- 76 Ultimate Westlife
- 80 **Real Life:** Behind The Scenes Of Pop

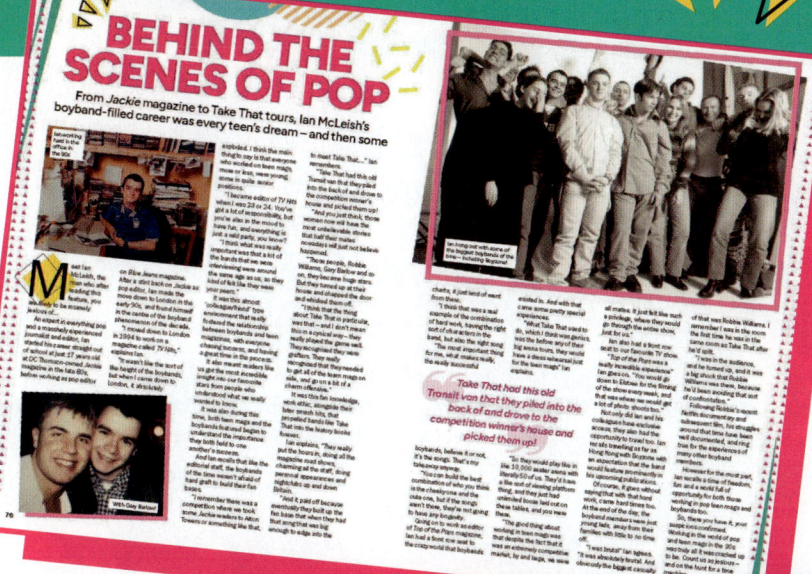

82 MID-LATE 1990s STATESIDE

- 84 Ultimate Backstreet Boys
- 88 **Real Life:** Dancing Queen
- 90 Ultimate NSYNC
- 92 Ultimate Hanson
- 94 Ultimate Boyz II Men

96 A NEW CHAPTER

- 98 Solo Success
- 103 10 Best Boyband Hits Of The 90s
- 104 Ultimate Gary Barlow
- 108 Take Five
- 112 Where Are They Now?
- 116 Ultimate Quiz
- 120 **Pin-up:** Take That
- 122 Behind The Hits!
- 124 **Pin-up:** Backstreet Boys
- 126 **Real Life:** Meet The Boyband Hit-Maker

Editor: Susan Watson **Head of Production:** Pete McDonald **Head of Design:** Jaclyn Bryson
Features Editor: Meghan McCormack **Feature Writers:** Susan Watson, Laura Coventry, Sue Dando, Sophie McVinnie, Mairi Hughes, Claire Macaulay, Alison James, Kirsty Nutkins, Marion Nixon **Thanks to the DC Thomson Archive Team:** Barry Sullivan, Niamh Quinn
Images: DCT Archive and Shutterstock unless otherwise stated.

Published in the UK by DC Thomson & Co Ltd, Dundee, Glasgow and London. © DC Thomson & Co Ltd, 2025. Registered Office: DC Thomson & Co Ltd, Courier Buildings, 2 Albert Square, Dundee, Scotland, DD1 9QJ. Distributed by Frontline Ltd, Stuart House, St John's St, Peterborough, Cambridgeshire PE1 5DD. Tel: +44 (0) 1733 555161. Website: www.frontlinedistribution.co.uk. Export distribution (excluding AU and NZ) Seymour Distribution Ltd, 2 East Poultry Avenue, London EC1A 9PT. Tel: +44(0)20 7429 4000. Fax: +44(0)20 7429 4001. Website: www.seymour.co.uk. EU Representative Office: DC Thomson & Co Ltd, c/o Findmypast Ireland, Irishtown, Athlone, Co. Westmeath, N37 XP52. Editorial communications to "Ultimate 90s Boybands", 2 Albert Square, Dundee DD1 1DD. Ultimate 90s Boybands is a member of IPSO (the Independent Press Standards Organisation), which regulates the UK's newspaper, magazine, and digital news industry. We abide by the Editors' Code of Practice and are committed to upholding the highest standards of journalism. If you think that we have not met those standards and want to make a complaint, please contact readerseditor@dcthomson.co.uk or Readers Editor, Ultimate 90s Boybands, 2 Albert Square, Dundee, Scotland, DD1 9QJ. If we are unable to resolve your complaint, or if you would like more information about IPSO or the Editors' Code, contact IPSO on 0300 123 2220 or visit www.ipso.co.uk

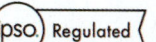 

THE EARLY YEARS

Part one: ULTIMATE TAKE THAT

From an ad in a newspaper to sold-out arenas, Take That's story proves dreams – and chart success – really do come true

THE NAME GAME
They were originally called Kick It and then The Cutest Crush, before Take That was chosen. In 2019 Mark revealed the band always disliked the name.

The band conquered teen hearts everywhere

Fresh-faced and funky, the boys in 1991

It was 'the greatest day' of their lives, when five Mancunian lads were chosen to form a UK boyband by Nigel Martin-Smith. The music producer had been inspired by the success of New Kids On The Block in the States and believed the UK music industry deserved an equivalent. So, after being introduced to young singer-songwriter Gary Barlow, Nigel placed an advert in local press, inviting "men who could sing and dance" to an open audition. That was when Howard Donald, Jason Orange, Mark Owen and Robbie Williams were recruited.

Like many manufactured pop bands of the 90s, Take That's members came from humble beginnings and their boy-next-door good looks were exactly what Martin-Smith was looking for when, unbeknownst to him, he formed one of the biggest boybands to ever come out of the UK.

However, their chart success did not happen overnight. Debut single *Do What You Like* charted in 1991 at number 82, follow-up single *Promises* went to number 38, and third release *Once You've Tasted Love* entered at 47.

Then everything changes… There is a breakthrough. *It Only Takes a Minute* charted at number seven. It was the first (of around 20) top 10 hits for the band. Four of them were back-to-back number ones in 1993-1994.

Take That-mania quickly spread across the UK and most teenage girls were swept up in it, following the band around the country, buying their singles and going to live gigs.

As we would later learn, many other UK boybands would form in the wake of Take That's early success.

Rivals would offer music, members and styles to suit every teenage girls' taste, but none would eclipse the success of this legendary boyband. ▶▶

DID YOU KNOW?

For *Relight My Fire* in 1993, the band teamed up with legendary Scottish singer, Lulu. Last year, the boys surprised the singer on stage to perform the hit song live on the last tour of her 60-year music career!

The band revved up the charts in the early 90s

TAKE THAT TOP 10

- It Only Takes A Minute (1992)
- A Million Love Songs (1992)
- Could It Be Magic? (1992)
- Why Can't I Wake Up With You (1993)
- Pray (1993)
- Relight My Fire (1993)
- Babe (1993)
- Everything Changes (1994)
- Love Ain't Here Anymore (1994)
- Sure (1994)

ICONIC

1992
DEBUT ALBUM
Reaching number 2 in the UK album chart, the band's debut album *Take That & Party* was a huge success. It stayed in the album chart for more than a year!

1994
RECOGNITION FOR GARY
As well as Take That winning a string of awards within their first few years of forming, lead singer Gary Barlow was recognised for his songwriting talents too. In 1994, Gary won an Ivor Novello Award for Songwriter of The Year. And that was before the band had even released number one hits

They ruled the charts – and our hearts

MOMENTS

Back for Good and Never Forget in 1995 and How Deep Is Your Love? in 1996.

1994
BIG CHANGES
In 1994, it was a first for Take That as Robbie sung the lead vocals on Everything Changes. The song, written by Gary, became Take That's fourth number one single. Interestingly, it was the only track on which Robbie sung lead.

1995
BIGGEST HIT
Take That's most successful track in terms of sales was 1995's Back For Good, one of the best-selling singles in UK history and one of the most beloved among fans.

Robbie sung the lead vocals on Everything Changes

SMASH HIT SUCCESS

Accepting an award at the 1994 Brits

SILVER CLEF AWARD
The band picked up the award for Best Newcomer in 1993.

BRIT AWARDS
TT won Brit Awards for British Single of The Year for Could It Be Magic in 1993 and for Pray in 1994. In 1994, they also took home the British Video of The Year award for Pray in 1994.

MTV EUROPE MUSIC AWARDS
As well as winning Best Group at the EMAs in 1994, the band were also picked up the International Viewers' Choice Award for Babe.

IVOR NOVELLO AWARD
Awarded to the band for Best Contemporary Song fof 1994 for Pray.

At the Brit Awards launch party in 1993

Part two on p60

A MILLION LOVE SONGS BY SPECIAL DELIVERY!

Anita Jayne Morrissey got the surprise of her life when her boyband heartthrob Gary Barlow crashed her wedding...

Anita Jayne will 'never forget' the shock!

FEATURE WRITER: ALISON JAMES

It was a perfect May evening in 2015 at the stately Knowsley Hall in Cheshire. The chandeliers sparkled, Champagne flowed and life-long Take That fan Anita Jayne Morrissey had just married the love of her life, Alex. But just when she thought the day couldn't get any better, in walked Gary Barlow. Yes, that Gary Barlow. The Take That superstar and, after Alex, the man of Anita Jayne's dreams. She sank to the floor in her white satin gown as Gary – walking past the Gary Barlow tribute act she and Alex had booked for the wedding entertainment – approached her, mic in hand, singing Take That's 1992 hit *A Million Love Songs*.

"I couldn't believe my eyes," she recalls. "Gary took my hands, pulled me up and hugged me. I was crying with happiness. I'm actually crying now just thinking about it. It was like something from a movie. One minute Alex and I were just dancing, and the next, Gary Barlow was singing to us! I thought I was hallucinating.

"It was the best day ever. Firstly because it was my wedding day, and secondly, there was Gary Barlow – superstar and the man I'd been a massive fan of for over 20 years – actually singing at our wedding. I will never, ever forget it."

In January 2015 Gary had announced, via social media, his intention to sing at the weddings of five of his fans. He invited fans to 'stalk' him on Twitter in order to be considered, specifying that he was looking for 'HUGE fans'. They didn't come much bigger than sales executive Anita Jayne, then 34. She'd first fallen for Take That as a 12-year-old in the early 1990s, buying their records and every teen mag they featured in, and watching every TV performance.

Within a few years, she was going to see them perform live whenever she could. And there was more. The band were based in Manchester and, being a Manchester girl, Anita Jayne would often hang out outside their homes with other superfans, hoping to catch a glimpse of her idols and maybe even get a wave or a hello or a quick pic.

When Take That split in 1996, Anita Jayne was so distraught she wasn't able to go to school for a week. When they announced they were reforming nine years later, she camped out for tickets for hours. Huge fan? Anita Jayne was in a class of her own.

Well before Gary's announcement, Anita Jayne's sister had contacted him asking if he'd sing at the wedding.

"She'd been tweeting him every day for about a year-and-a-half – since we'd started planning the big day, in fact. Gary knew who I was as I'd been to so many concerts and stuff. Shortly before he tweeted his announcement about his intention to sing at a few fans' weddings, Gary tweeted my fellow Take That fan, Kalisha, telling her he intended to come to mine but swearing her to secrecy. He'd already decided to come to our wedding! Maybe it was my wedding that had even given him the idea!"

Several months of subterfuge followed. Oblivious

Gary

Mark

Howard

Anita Jayne, Alex and Gary on the couple's big day

HAPPY ANNIVERSARY!

Gary Barlow's presence at their wedding obviously brought Anita Jayne and Alex good luck as they recently celebrated their 10th anniversary and are happier than ever – even though there is another man in Anita Jayne's life!

"Alex is very tolerant of my passion for Gary and Take That," says Anita Jayne.

"He's known about my love for the band for a long time. My family lost no time in telling him how obsessed I was when we got together but I don't think he quite 'got' it until he saw how ecstatic I was when Take That reformed in 2005.

"He couldn't believe how I was willing to camp out to get tickets and wanted to go to as many concerts as I could. It's the same now – on their most recent tour I saw them several times and travelled to different cities to do so.

"Alex knows it makes me happy and so he's willing to indulge me. To be honest, though, he doesn't have much choice!"

The other man in her life!

to the fact that Gary would be surprising her at the wedding, Anita Jayne continued to message him, pleading her case and asking him to come. Finally, Gary contacted her to tell her he was so sorry but he wouldn't be able to because he was performing the same evening. It was a not-so-little white lie!

"Once I'd heard that, I accepted he wouldn't be there. I was very disappointed but it meant Alex and I could get on with planning our wedding. As the real Gary Barlow couldn't be there, we booked a great Gary tribute act, Dan Hadfield. Little did I know that both Dan – and Alex – knew that the real Gary would be coming! Dan had to know so he'd be able to harmonise with Gary when Gary showed up.

"On the morning of the wedding, Gary sent me a message, wishing me and Alex a great day and again apologising for not being able to be there. Yet 10 or so hours later, there he was! Could it be magic? It so was!"

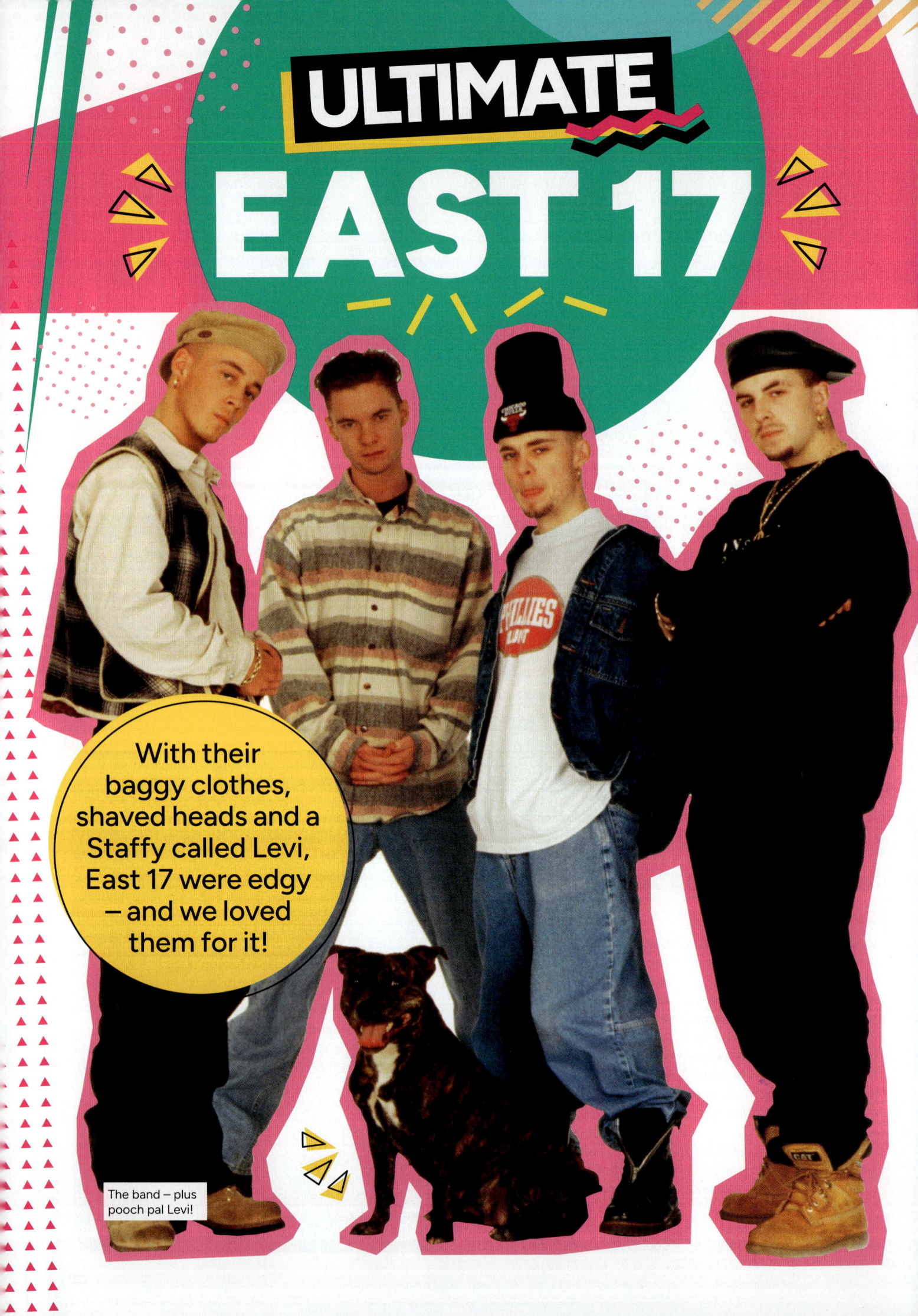

ULTIMATE EAST 17

With their baggy clothes, shaved heads and a Staffy called Levi, East 17 were edgy – and we loved them for it!

The band – plus pooch pal Levi!

The band brought the streets to the stage

When East 17 formed in 1991, they offered teenage pop fans an alternative vibe – and sound – to the squeaky clean image of the original boyband.

Dressed in combat trousers, with shaved heads, skip caps and tattoos, and hailing from east London, Brian Harvey, Tony Mortimer, Terry Coldwell and John Hendy were edgy – and we loved them for it!

The four-piece were formed by Tom Watkins (who also managed pop trio Bros) and burst onto the UK music scene with their unqiue style of music.

They took influences from pop, R'n'B and hip-hop and their tracks were a mix of ballads and upbeat songs that featured Brian's instantly-recognisable strong vocals, often followed by a rhythmic rap from Tony.

Interestingly, it was originally talented songwriter Tony and backing vocalist John who were chosen to be the singers of the band, while pals Brian and Terry would be the dancers.

But when they heard Brian singing during a recording session, he was quickly promoted to lead vocalist. *House Of Love* was their first single to enter the top 10 and sold 600,000 copies in 1992. A debut album, *Walthamstow*, followed the next year and it charted at number one.

In total, *East 17* had 18 top 20 tracks – including *It's Alright*, *Steam*, *Deep, Hold My Body Tight* and of course 1994 Christmas number one *Stay Another Day* – and four top 10 albums. For five years they dominated the charts with hit after hit. They toured extensively in the 90s achieving around 20 million record sales across the world. Fans used to dress in camouflage combat trousers in tribute to their edgy style.

At one point they were considered to be one of the biggest bands in the 1990s and one of the most influential boybands of their generation.

However, it all came to a sudden end in 1997 when Brian admitted to using drugs. The tabloid press splashed the story on the front cover. This admission resulted in the four-piece splitting up in what was one of the most controversial boyband break-ups of the decade. ▶▶

Brian had a high-profile romance with actress Daniella Westbrook

DID YOU KNOW?

East 17 – often abbrievated to E17 – were named after the postal district in London from where the lads hailed. The E17 postcode covers Walthamstow, Upper Walthamsow and Waltham Forest in East London. It is known for its commuity spirit and arts scene.

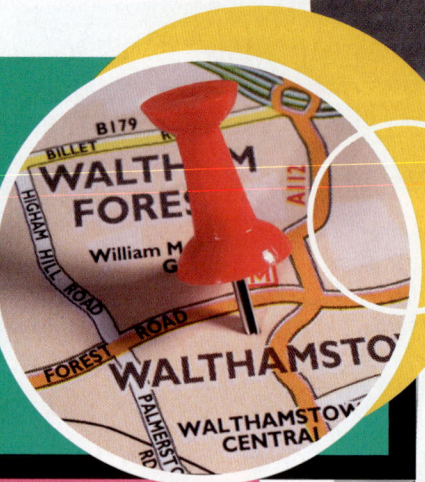

EAST 17 TOP 10

- House Of Love (1992)
- Deep (1993)
- It's Alright (1994)
- Around The World (1994)
- Steam (1994)
- Stay Another Day (1994)
- Let It Rain (1995)
- Thunder (1995)
- Do You Still? (1996)
- If You Ever (1996)

ICONIC

1993
DEBUT HIT
East 17's first album *Walthamstow* was named after their hometown in east London and featured John's dog Levi on the cover. It put the East End town – and band – on the map, as it shot to number one.

1994
CHRISTMAS SUCCESS
Stay Another Day was East 17's biggest hit and became the Christmas number one in 1994. The boys were dressed in their iconic white fur-lined puffa coats for the music video. The ballad, which was written by Tony about the death of his brother, remained at the top spot for five weeks.

1995
UP ALL NIGHT
The band release their third studio album, the last to feature all original East 17 members.

East 17 proved that pop didn't need polish

From left, Brian, John, Tony and Terry

MOMENTS

1996
GABRIELLE DUET
They team up with the patch-wearing pop diva for *If You Ever*. It charts at number two.

1997
CONTROVERSIAL SPLIT
Brian was dismissed after controversial drug comments. The group disbanded shortly after amid falling sales.

> **DID YOU KNOW?**
>
> After the split in 1997, they reformed again just a year later as E-17 without main songwriter Tony but with Brian reinstated. However, new album *Resurrection* was a flop and they disbanded once more. Since then, they have continued to perform with different line-ups.

SMASH HIT SUCCESS

MTV Award winners in 1995

MERCURY MUSIC PRIZE
In 1993, their debut album *Walthamstow* was nominated for the prestigious music award.

BRAVO OTTO AWARDS
East 17 won Best Pop Band Award at the Otto awards organised by German magazine *Bravo*.

IVOR NOVELLO AWARD
Delighted to be nominated for Best British Single for *Stay Another Day* in 1994.

SMASH HITS POLL WINNERS PARTY AWARDS
In the running for Best Single (for *If You Ever*) and Best British Group at the Poll Winners Party.

MTV EUROPE MUSIC AWARDS
Named Best Dance Group in Paris at the EMAs in 1995.

Heavenly harmonies

ULTIMATE BOYZONE

The hair gel! The ballads! The brotherhood! Revisit the rollercoaster journey of the one and only Boyzone

DID YOU KNOW?
The band reunited once more for their 2025 documentary *Boyzone: No Matter What*. Ronan Keating explained that this behind-the-scenes look, featuring new footage and interviews wasn't the "typical" boyband documentary. Keith Duffy likened the experience to a counselling session.

The band, from left, Ronan, Mikey, Stephen, Shane and Keith

They stumbled on live TV before soaring in the charts

Boyzone were formed by Louis Walsh as Ireland's answer to Take That. The original line-up consisted of Ronan Keating, Stephen Gately, Shane Lynch, Keith Duffy, Mark Walton and Richie Rock, but shortly after the band formed, Walton and Rock stepped away, with Mikey Graham joining the gang to complete the band we know today.

The boys had a rocky start to their career with their endearing debut performance. 'That' performance on RTÉ's *The Late Late Show* was critically panned – something we can forgive Boyzone for, given they only found out they were all actually in the band the night before!

Happily, we soon learned that we 'loved them for a reason' as the group went on to achieve six UK number one singles, and nine in Ireland, with over 25 million records being sold worldwide. Boyzone were named the second most successful boyband in Britain after Take That by the Official Charts Company in 2012.

In a landmark revelation, Stephen Gately publicly came out as gay in 1999, opening up important conversations about sexuality. He became the first openly gay members of a major boyband, and the overwhelmingly positive response highlighted the increasing LGBTQ+ support in the UK and Ireland.

After many harmonies and dance routines, the band disbanded in 2000 before getting back together in 2007. Sadly, the good times didn't last as Stephen Gately tragically passed away in 2009 from a congenital heart defect.

The band continued to honour his legacy and wrapped up for good in 2019, touring with final album *Thank You & Goodnight*, cementing their place in charts and hearts. ▶▶

DID YOU KNOW?

Shane is a professional racing driver, competing regularly in the British Touring Car Championship!

BOYZONE TOP 10

- Love Me For a Reason (1994)
- Father and Son (1995)
- Words (1996)
- Baby Can I Hold You/ Shooting Star (1997)
- Picture of You (1997)
- I Love The Way You Love Me (1998)
- No Matter What (1998)
- Every Day I Love You (1999)
- You Needed Me (1999)
- When The Going Gets Tough (1999)

Their cheeky personas made us all melt!

ICONIC

1993
THE LATE LATE SHOW APPEARANCE
Boyzone's first performance didn't see them singing at all, instead performing a dance they had half an hour to prepare in the dressing room!

1997
PICTURE OF YOU
This track became the main theme for *Bean: The Ultimate Disaster Movie*, and comedic powerhouse Rowan Atkinson made an appearance in the music video too!

1998
NO MATTER WHAT
Their reimagining of this *Whistle Down the Wind* track was a huge hit, and their only song to chart in America.

1999
MTV EUROPE MUSIC AWARDS
Lead singer Ronan hosted the

The band enjoyed hit after hit

MOMENTS

MTV Music Awards when they were held in Dublin, putting Boyzone on the map internationally.

2010
GAVE IT ALL AWAY
After Stephen's heartbreaking death at 33, Boyzone paid tribute to their friend with this track, which included Gately's vocals and an emotional music video.

Stephen Gately

Irish charm and soulful tunes

SMASH HIT SUCCESS

At the MTV Europe Awards in 1996

BRIT AWARDS
The band took home Best International Single for *No Matter What* in 1998 and *When the Going Gets Tough* in 1999, as well as Best International Group that same year.

MTV EUROPE MUSIC AWARDS
The Irish sensations received nominations for Best Pop in 1998 and 1999, taking home Best UK & Ireland Act in 1999.

IVOR NOVELLO AWARD
Picture of You from the *Bean* movie won Best Contemporary Song in 1998.

UK SMASH HITS POLL
They swept the board in 1996 with six top spots. This poll was fan-voted, showing the band's mass appeal!

16 TOP FIVE SINGLES
In a feat that no boyband of the time had achieved, Boyzone broke records with 16 consecutive top five singles in the UK chart.

Performing at the Brits in 1999

NSYNC

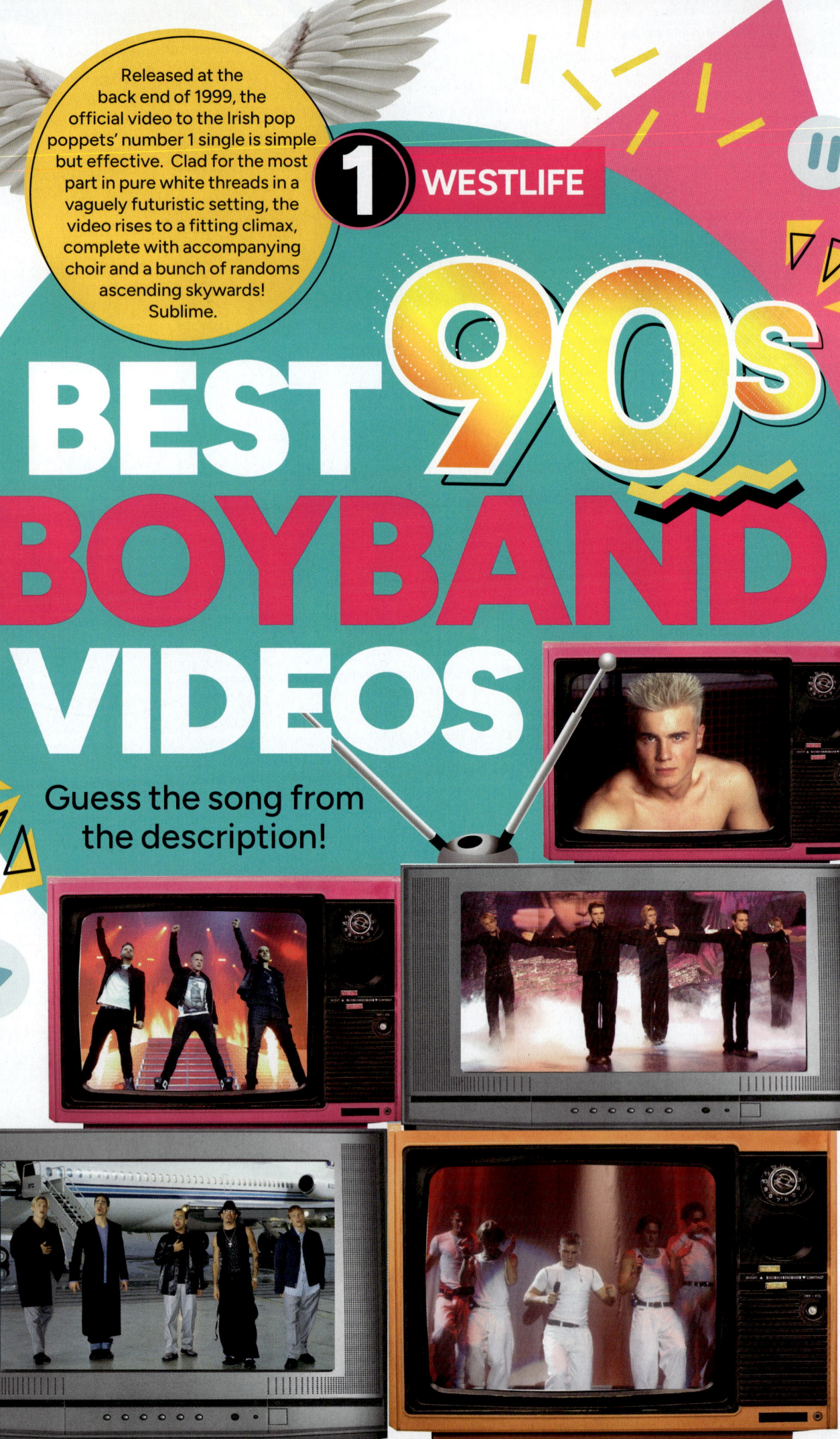

BEST 90s BOYBAND VIDEOS

Guess the song from the description!

1 WESTLIFE

Released at the back end of 1999, the official video to the Irish pop poppets' number 1 single is simple but effective. Clad for the most part in pure white threads in a vaguely futuristic setting, the video rises to a fitting climax, complete with accompanying choir and a bunch of randoms ascending skywards! Sublime.

2 BOYZONE

The video for arguably Boyzone's most beloved song had everything. Hot air balloons! A mysterious bendy cool girl! Ronan Keating's magnificent sideburns! The band all dressed in white and looking swarthy and enunciating to perfection! And of course, Stephen Gateley's soaring vocals. No wonder the single got to number one in 1998. It's an absolute corker.

3 TAKE THAT

Not only a masterpiece in songwriting from the genius mind of Gary Barlow, but a masterstroke of nostalgia, this video pulls at the heartstrings from start to finish. From its photo montage of the boys as children at the beginning to reels of the fivesome as their fame soared, it's a wonderful flashback on a career that rose like a phoenix to the flame. And it's all the more poignant with the knowledge that it was the band's last song before Robbie left (blub!).

4 FIVE

The video for one of Five's biggest hits starts in a similar vein to the Britney Spears' classic ...Baby One More Time video. Set in a classroom of bored teenagers about to start an exam, a thumping rock beat begins, the boys appear onstage at the front of the school hall and away we go. Cue chairs flying and kids ripping their clothes off in a frenzy of youthful rebellion. Add in a rap from singers Jason "J" Brown and Richard "Abs" Breen and you've got yourself one of the coolest videos of the 90s.

5 EAST 17

The debate over whether this perennial festive favourite is actually a Christmas song will rage forevermore. However, one thing is true: the accompanying video is so festive it might as well include Father Christmas and a herd of reindeer. But it doesn't. Instead, the angelic-looking London quartet, known for not being all that angelic, are clad in white fluffy parkas and floating around in the ether, embracing the Christmassy vibe wholeheartedly. Why, there's even dodgy fake snow superimposed on the video. Iconic.

6 BACKSTREET BOYS

The boys' video for their biggest UK hit was mostly shot at Los Angeles International Airport, a real coup for them as, at the time, filming wasn't allowed. The boys made the most of their stunt, wandering through the departure lounge and spending much of the four minutes grooving on the runway in perfectly styled co-ords in front of a private jet (quite how much they paid for said borrowed plane's cameo is neither here nor there). Oh, and escalators feature. Lots and lots of escalators...

Answers: 1. Westlife: Flying Without Wings. 2. Boyzone: No Matter What. 3. Take That: Never Forget. 4. Five: Everybody Get Up. 5. East 17: Stay Another Day. 6. Backstreet Boys: I Want It That Way.

BEHIND THE SCENES OF

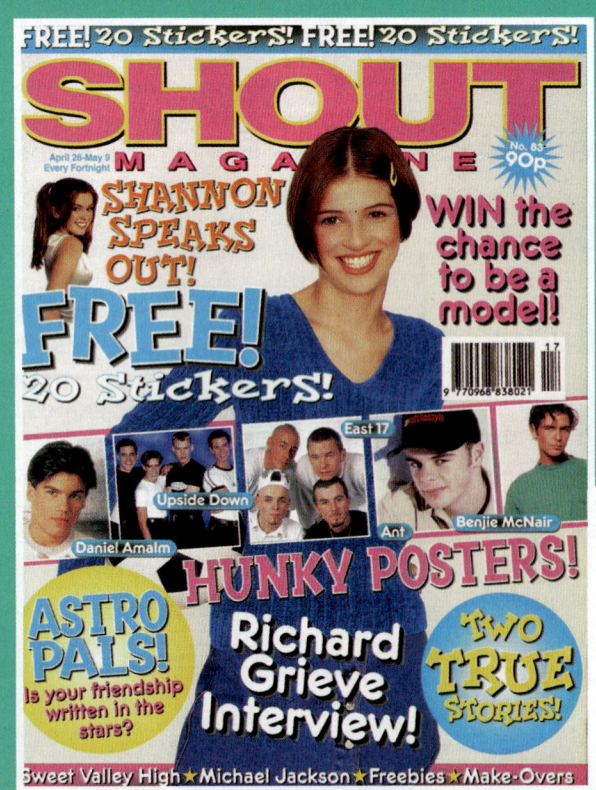

SHOUT

Let's reminisce and meet some of the talent behind our favourite 90s teen magazine…

Cast your mind back to a time before Instagram, TikTok, Facebook, and the whole world wasn't just a mere tap away. Algorithms weren't a thing, and there wasn't a sea of trends that moved so quickly, you'd blink and miss 'em.

If you were a teen in the 90s, the likelihood is that it was a walk along to your local newsagent that was the equivalent of stepping inside a whole other world beyond your wildest dreams – the world of pop!

Hands up if you spent your pocket money on the likes of *Shout, Bliss* and *Mizz*? I will safely assume all our hands are up. Picking up your favourite mag was guaranteed to give you an insight like no other into your favourite stars of the day – most notably, boybands.

Only on these coveted pages could you find out what Jason Orange really liked for his tea, you know, should he ever stop by, discover you're his one true love, and you had to send your mum to the shops for something special.

Only through the glossy photographs and pop quizzes could you find out which band you were truly destined to follow for the rest of your days – East 17 or Five? No matter which boyband camp you sat in, teen magazines in the 90s championed their readers' tastes like no other platform had done before.

They had the inside scoop, they knew the people to talk to and the questions to ask that would appeal to their readers and give them a sense of belonging.

They truly took their readers along on an incredible ride, and with them, it can be argued, gave boybands a platform to capitalise on their growing success and have that unique and direct line with their fans.

It helps that the talented journalists and editors working on these magazines were not far off the ages of the readers themselves, as well as the stars and boybands they covered.

They knew exactly what their readers wanted, and by creating strong relationships with the stars, could offer it up on a plate for readers to pore over week after week.

For any boyband mega fan, working on a teen mag in the 90s was the ultimate career goal.

So before we take you on a trip down memory lane on *Shout* mag – how lucky are we to have access to the archives? – let's meet the talented brains behind the pages who brought us the news we coveted in the decade of boybands… ▶▶

THIS WAS THEIR BREAD & BUTTER!

Jackie Brown

Jackie Brown, a highly regarded magazine editor from Kirkcaldy, was the powerhouse behind the launch of *Shout* magazine in the early 90s.

"I worked on *Jackie* (magazine) in the 80s, I was the pop editor in 84/85," Jackie recalls.

"*Jackie* was coming to an end, not because it wasn't good, but when we spoke to the girls, they didn't want to read a magazine that their grannies had read."

With a huge wealth of experience behind her, Jackie knew that there was a place in the market for a magazine that had a similar ethos but had a fresh new look. And so, with Jackie's idea, *Shout* magazine was born in 1993.

"It was built on boybands, really. It was built on boybands and soap stars, because at the time, *Neighbours* and *Home and Away* were massive. I worked out if we got writers in Australia… then we were the magazine in the know."

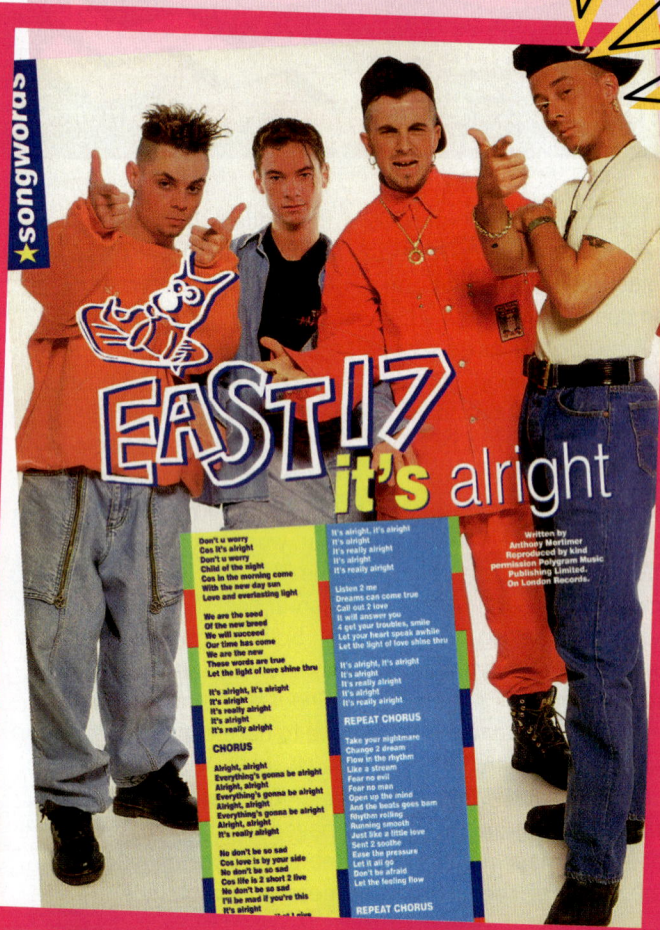

"*Jackie* finished in 93 and *Shout* launched in 93, we literally switched the presses."

With the influx of boybands on the scene, *Shout* magazine used the opportunity to become the place to be for fans to find out anything they wanted to know. And on the flip side, boybands knew the power of teen magazines, too.

"They weren't daft. They knew. They knew what us putting them on the cover meant" Jackie explains.

"Take That gave us a gold disc in recognition of our support!

"We sold it on eBay, and we gave the money to charity."

To give an idea of scale, when *Shout* launched, Jackie recalls they were selling around 300,000 copies a fortnight. That's a lot of fan eyes for boybands to bask in!

"Boybands knew that was their bread and butter. And it was still in the days of actual physical transparencies!" Jackie explains.

"They would do a photo shoot, and the teen mags would all get an exclusive look from that. *Just 17* would get one, *Mizz* would get one, *Shout* would get one, *Bliss*, *Top of the Pops* magazine, we'd all get an exclusive picture….

"A lot of girls at that time, because they didn't have phones, no access to anything, they would buy a magazine for that one picture that they hadn't seen."

SO MUCH GOING ON!

Tracey, left, and Lucy

Talented journalists Tracey Steele and Lucy Crichton worked alongside Jackie on *Shout* in the early 90s and look back on their time spent there fondly.

"It was just an amazing, amazing experience" Tracey recalls.

"There was always stuff going on in the office. It was exciting. People were always going down to London to do sessions. I mean, we tasted a bit of that on *Jackie* (magazine) as well."

Shout magazine was based in Dundee, at DC Thomson headquarters in Meadowside. However, even with frequent staff trips to London, stars of the time regularly made the trip to the offices.

Tracey recalls, "Anybody could have walked in, and you would just be like, alright? You know, because you it was just part of your day-to-day thing."

It's hard to imagine where Teams and Zoom calls don't exist to make chats like this possible, but journalists like Tracey and Lucy at the time persevered with what they had to ensure they brought their readers their regular dose of boyband gossip and news.

"In our office, there were two phones" Lucy remembers. "One was on the editor's desk, and the other one was a booth!

"I loved it. It really was an absolute dream. No matter what you were doing on the magazine, there was just a brilliant vibe. The floor was buzzing. You had so many people, all about your age."

WHY CAN'T I WAKE UP WITH YOU

Oh, I can't decide if I should read or think
I'll keep an open mind, 'til the day sets in
Hear you call me (hear you call me, hear you call me)
I'm so willing to call back (willing to call back)
Hear you thinking (hear you thinking, hear you thinking)
Hope you hear me thinking too

CHORUS
Why can't I wake up with you (why can't I wake up with you)
So you're there when I open my eyes (there when I open my eyes)
Baby why can't I wake up with you (why can't I wake up with you)
You're my life (my love)
Ooh, ooh, you're my life

Feel alive, so I'll just begin (just begin)
Yeah to read my mind, before you ring me (before you ring)
Hear you thinking, hear you thinking
Hope you hear me thinking too, whoah

REPEAT CHORUS

So good to be near you (so good to be near you)
So dark when you walk from my side (walk from my side)
Baby why can't I wake up with you
You're my life (you're my life)
You're my life

Hear you thinking, yeah (hear you thinking)
Hope you hear me thinking too
Darling, ooh
Why can't I wake up with you
You're there when I open my eyes
Why can't I wake up with you
My love
Why can't I wake up with you
There when I open my eyes
Why can't I wake up with you
(ad lib to fade)

Written by Gary Barlow
Reproduced by kind permission EMI Virgin Music Ltd.
On R.C.A. Records.

And with such passion and fun-loving spirit, it's clear to see why the likes of *Shout* magazine thrived in the 1990s, and why a job there was so enviable! So without further ado, pop on your chosen boyband playlist, and let's take a step back in time and enjoy the incredible insights the likes of Jackie, Tracey, Lucy and their colleagues curated for us fans, 30 years ago... ▶▶

5 Go Mad In PARIS

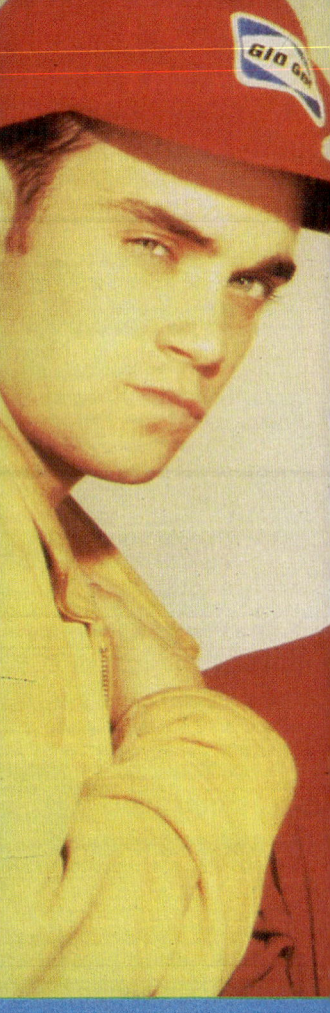

Take a trip round Paris in the hands of five of the most able tour guides — Take That!

On a beautiful but rather chilly day at 2pm Take That are about to discover Paris for the first time. As we speak, Howard is lying on a bed waiting for his turn to be made-up and Jason is already in the hands of French make-up girl Valerie. The other three have disappeared to their rooms, getting ready for the big day ahead.

Robbie is the first one to make it into the hotel lobby. He's carrying a notepad and whenever anyone speaks to him in French, he writes it down.

"At school I used to sit at the back of the class mucking around, especially in the French class. Now I'm here in Paris, how am I going to speak to those girls out there?"

As it turns out, some girls have already turned up in front of the hotel hoping to spot the boys, and the sight of Robbie seems to send them into a frenzy. "Let's go out and talk to them," he says, and as he walks out to meet the fans he's handed a small piece of paper that reads, "Will you marry me?" Things are looking up for Take That today . . .

Each time another member of the band appears, the French fans go wild.

"I can't believe it, this one is even more gorgeous than the last one," screams one girl, in English!

THE INTERVIEWS

The boys laugh, smile for the souvenir snaps and all pile into a massive limo. Gay Paree, here we come . . .

As the car drives along the River Seine, the boys gaze out the windows taking in the sights. "Paris is beautiful," muses Howard. ". . . But the girls are even better," says Mark, which cracks everyone up.

First stop is a French radio station where they are being interviewed and asked such fascinating questions as, "Where do you come from? How did you meet? Where does the name of the band come from?"

On Manchester, they say, "We've never spent any time away from it to this day, really." As it turns out this is a bit of a fib 'cos Take That have just returned from a promotional trip to Spain.

They found Madrid a bit upsetting — supposedly some of them got lost one evening in one of the seediest parts of town and nearly got mugged, but nobody wants to talk about their experience. Jason is determined to return though and is learning to speak Spanish at the moment.

Having done a bit of sight-seeing, horse-riding on a roundabout (bizarre as it may sound), window shopping, posing on a statue and going for some croissants in a groovy Parisian café, the lads are ready for their first major commitment of the afternoon: they're to be interviewed by five French fans for a local teenage mag.

We listened in to what they said, and found them in a rather playful mood . . .

CHILDHOOD

JASON: "We spent our teenage years in Manchester. We all started dancing in the local youth clubs when we were about 13 and then we decided to form a band. We're still trying!"

MARK: "We had some great times back then. Our teenage years were about the same as anyone else's, y'know, hanging out with your mates, spending afternoons in the park trying to meet as many girls as possible. We weren't very good at school, that was the only bad bit about being teenagers."

GARY: "I had a good time at school. Fell in love during the first year . . ."

ROBBIE: ". . . and the second year, and the third!"

MARK: "I was mad about football then, I even thought about becoming a professional player. I played for quite a few good clubs round my area, but whenever some coaches would come and see me play to see if I was worth signing, I would get very nervous and play really badly.

Eventually I gave it up 'cos I was too small anyway. When I wasn't playing football, I would spend my time practising my Elvis impersonations in front of the mirror."

GARY: "I started playing piano at the age of 10, I was given keyboards for Christmas and I taught myself, more or less. I started playing piano professionally when I was 11, playing in pubs and restaurants around my area."

ROBBIE: "I was born in Ireland *(don't believe everything you read, as Robbie himself says, 'Usually whenever my lips are moving, it means I'm lying')* — I moved to England when I was 10, then I spent my teenage years at military school." (Another lie, possibly!)

JOBS FOR THE BOYS

GARY: "I don't think I could have done anything else other than this."

JASON: "I think we've been very lucky, 'cos we always liked dancing most of all. We've been quite lucky to have made it as a band, but we're still learning."

HOWARD: "I was rather good at music at school, I played the trumpet and I'm learning the guitar now. My parents were quite musical too . . ."

MARK: ". . . yeah, his mum is Madonna and his dad is Axl Rose!"

ROBBIE: "I wanted to be famous by any means possible. Whether it was by playing football, singing or doing an advert for baked beans. Well, I suppose I've nearly succeeded."

MARK: "What do you mean, you're the most famous person I know!"
ROBBIE: "Even more famous than God!"
GARY: "But our success didn't all happen at once. We knew we'd make it one day though, 'cos we all got on really well, right from the start. I'm glad that our success took time, 'cos it makes us appreciate what we have now. My mother always used to say to me, 'Get a proper job'."

And what does she say now?
GARY: "Get a proper job!"

Gary, where do you get the inspiration for your songwriting?

ROBBIE: "From me!"
GARY: "From everywhere, really. From reading, listening to Robbie's sorrows, from stories your mates tell you, from my own personal experiences."

How do the others contribute?
ALL: "We don't!"
HOWARD: "Jason and I do the choreography, and we all sing on the album, of course. Whenever one of us has an idea for a song we bring it to Gary."
ROBBIE: "I play the triangle, me!"
MARK: "We're all sort of playing on the album in places, but it's still at a learning stage. Howard plays a bit of keyboard, Jason plays a bit of guitar . . . and I play football!"

GIRLFRIENDS

JASON: "I've got too many, I'm going a bit crazy at the moment! I can't control myself. It's difficult to have a serious relationship 'cos we're always so busy. There are so many pretty girls to meet, so watch out!"
HOWARD: "We're young lads. It would be hard to commit yourself to someone 'cos we're never there, it would be a real mess. It just doesn't work when you're so far away from each other all the time and it's not fair on your partner."

MARK: "Well, personally, I'm married and I've got seven kids!"
ROBBIE: "I'm desperately looking for a girlfriend, especially since I'm in romantic Paris."

THE PERSONAL STUFF!

Describe each other in three words . . .
GARY: "Robbie is funny, chatty and a liar!"
HOWARD: "Gary is serious, clever and sincere."
MARK: "Howard is sensible, romantic and has a very dry sense of humour." *(That's more than three words!)*
JASON: "Mark is understanding, inquisitive and caring."
ROBBIE: "Jason is a perfectionist, interesting, and always ready to stand up for the others."

Your wildest dream . . .
GARY: "A night out in Paris."
JASON: "To see the world and meet everyone."
MARK: "To get married one day and have lots of kids."
HOWARD: "To get married, have kids and spend lots of time with my mum who's really encouraged me throughout my career." *(Awww)*
ROBBIE: "I want to win a cup-winner's medal!"

What would you do if you were Prime Minister for a day?
JASON: "Try and help the problems in Somalia."
MARK: "Yeah, stop famine."
HOWARD: "Try and end unemployment."
GARY: "No more wars."
ROBBIE: "I would change my underwear."

How do you see yourself at 50?
MARK: "A grandfather — I want my children to have babies early!"
GARY: "I think I'll be living in Australia with 10 kids."
ROBBIE: "I honestly think I'll be dead!"
EVERYONE: "Oh, shut up Robbie!"

"I'M OBSESSED BY TAKE THAT"

We take a look at the effect Take That have had on some girls' lives . . .

Here at *Shout*, we know for a fact that there are an awful lot of Take That fans out there — we get sackloads of mail every fortnight to prove it! To some girls, though, Take That have become more than just another band. To them the lads have become an obsession — one which threatens to take control of their whole lives. Here are just some of those girls' true stories . . .

"I used to slag off all the people at school who loved Take That. I just did it because a couple of my friends said they were rubbish — I hadn't actually heard their music or seen them.

"Then, one day, I saw them on TV and couldn't believe it. They were gorgeous. Straight away I went out and bought their album and I've been playing it ever since! My friend Joanna, who I used to be really rotten to about Take That, was brilliant and lent me their video.

"When I asked Mum if I could have money for a concert ticket she said we couldn't afford it. I wouldn't speak to her for ages, I just stormed around the house or sat in my room crying. Eventually my dad (Mum and him are divorced) sent the money to the ticket office. I was so worried the tickets wouldn't turn up, I was late for school a couple of times because I was hanging around waiting for the post. The tickets arrived a week and a half later — I rang Joanna straight away to tell her!

"The concert was brilliant but I was so excited I can hardly remember any of it. For a week after it I didn't want to go out, I just wanted to sit and think about how it felt to see Mark and the others close up. Joanna still rings me up and we speak about that and nothing else.

"She fancies this lad she says looks like Gary Barlow, but he's not interested in her. His friend asked her out but she said no.

"I've never had a real boyfriend but I'm not bothered because I can't see any of the daft boys I know matching up to Mark Owen!"
Angela, 13.

"People don't understand how it feels when you love a band. "My best mate, Katie, got me into Take That and we bought tickets for their concert. The minute they hit the stage, I fell in love with them and since then I just keep getting more and more obsessed. I buy every magazine they're in and my bedroom walls are covered in posters.

"I hardly ever bother going out with my friends any more because there just doesn't seem to be any point. I'd rather look at my pictures and imagine how life would be if I knew the band. Gary's my favourite and I wrote him a personal letter telling him how much I love him and it broke my heart when I didn't get a reply.

"My friends don't understand how I feel and neither do my parents or my sister. They laugh at me and say I'll get over it. My sister drew on a poster I had of Gary on his own and I was so mad I grabbed her arm and started hitting her. Mum was really angry and told me to pull myself together and stop being so ridiculous. She says I'm ruining my life over someone I'll never meet and she threatened to tear down all my posters and throw out my album and video.

"I just wish people would understand how I feel. They might think it's just a stupid crush but I can't help it — it feels real to me. I can't imagine ever not feeling like this."
Katie, 14.

"I get really jealous when I hear of people who have met Take That. Why should they be so lucky, instead of me?

"My best friend, Julie, feels exactly the same way as I do about the band. We spend hours watching their video and talking about them. I couldn't be friends with anyone who didn't feel the way I do about Take That. What would be the point?

Push

"I went to see Take That a while ago and it was the best day of my life. I managed to push my way quite far down the front even though everyone was shouting and screaming. It was so packed and hot I could hardly breathe and I felt a bit sick but I was determined I was staying.

"After seeing the band live, I now realise just how much I love them.

"I've got three Take That scrapbooks where I stick stuff that's been in magazines and my favourite photos. I can sit for hours and look at them over and over again."
Naomi, 14.

"I live in the North of Scotland which means it's really difficult to go to any Take That concerts. That really bugs me because I like them just as much as anyone down South.

"I buy every magazine that mentions them, especially if there's a picture of Jason on his own. He's definitely the best-looking boy in the world.

"I dream about Jason all the time, probably because I kiss my favourite picture of him every night before I go to sleep.

"Sometimes I cry because everything just gets too much for me. I know deep down that it's hopeless but I just can't help the way I feel. I'd rather feel like this than not know about Take That.

Album

"I've got loads of Take That stuff — three books, all their singles, the album and the video. I've got a T-shirt but I don't wear it because I don't want to spoil it.

"My family say I'm boring and I talk about Take That all the time, but I don't care what they think.

"I had exams recently and I know I didn't study enough because I couldn't concentrate on anything but the band and I just ended up reading features about them. My mum and dad would go mad if they knew!

"Sometimes real life just seems so dull and boring. When I feel like that, I go and look through all my magazines, or watch my video and pretend I'm with Take That! Sometimes what I'm imagining just seems so much more real than what's actually going on in my life."
Emma, 13.

If any of these readers' stories sound just like you, you could be letting your obsession with Take That get out of hand . . .

JUST A CRUSH?

We know you've heard it a million times before, but I'm afraid we'll have to say it again . . . the way you're feeling is a crush. You can't fall 'in love' with someone you don't know, even when they're as good-looking as the Take That lads!

Before you can be in love with someone you have to get to know them properly. That means experiencing the bad bits as well as the good, because nobody's perfect!

'Real' boys have habits that bug you and say things which annoy you, but it's easy to build stars you've never met into perfect lads who would never do anything to put you off them.

This isn't real love, as we've said, but that doesn't make the feelings any less strong. Crushes can feel just as powerful (or even more so) as falling for a boy you actually know.

In fact, crushes are harder to cope with because you rarely get the chance to meet the person you're obsessed with. If you did, and you got to know them, you'd quickly realise that no way are they as perfect as you thought!

WHEN THE PROBLEMS START . . .

Having a crush on someone doesn't have to be a problem. Daydreaming about someone you really like is a brilliant way to spend some time and it's a natural part of growing up. The problems start when the crush takes over your life. If you'd rather shut yourself away in your room to stare at your Take That posters and listen to their album than go out with your mates and have fun, that's a sign that things are out of hand.

If this sounds like you, not only are you missing out on having a laugh with your friends, you're giving up the opportunity to meet boys — real boys who are within your reach!

GIVE THEM A CHANCE!

The lads you know might not be as good-looking as Take That-ers but (unless you're seriously unlucky!) they can't be all that bad!

You will meet someone you really like, but only if you give them a chance instead of automatically ruling them out because they aren't part of Take That!

When you do meet someone you really want to go out with, you'll realise that you can still like Take That — they just don't rule your life any more because you're too busy having fun!

What we're saying is, it's fine to dream about Take That but don't let it make you miserable. After all, Gary, Howard, Mark, Jason and Robbie would hate to think they'd had that effect!

KISS AND TELL!

Brace yourself for some saucy secrets as those bad boys Ally, Matthew, David and Tony talk about love!

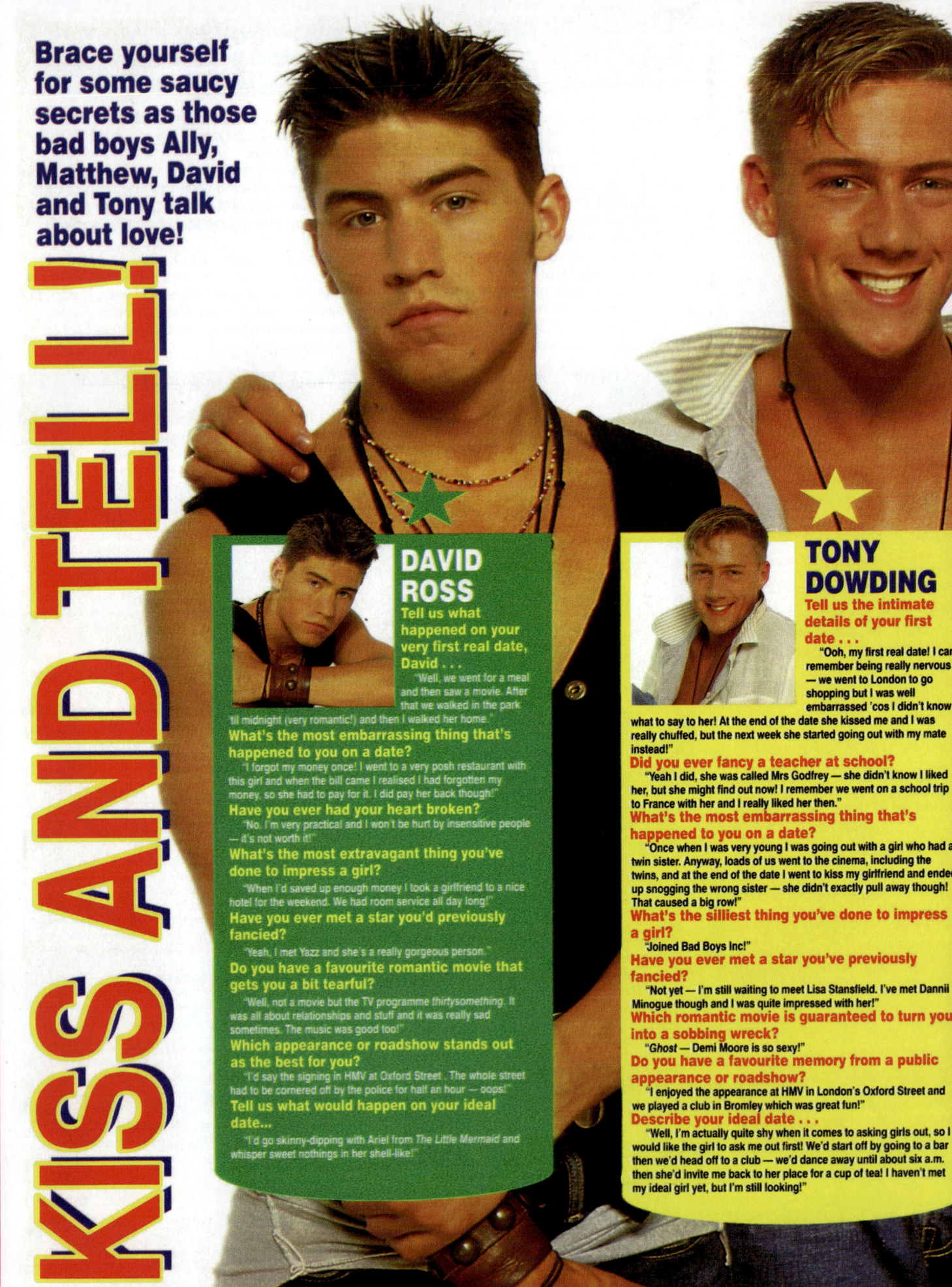

DAVID ROSS

Tell us what happened on your very first real date, David...
"Well, we went for a meal and then saw a movie. After that we walked in the park 'til midnight (very romantic!) and then I walked her home."

What's the most embarrassing thing that's happened to you on a date?
"I forgot my money once! I went to a very posh restaurant with this girl and when the bill came I realised I had forgotten my money, so she had to pay for it. I did pay her back though!"

Have you ever had your heart broken?
"No. I'm very practical and I won't be hurt by insensitive people — it's not worth it!"

What's the most extravagant thing you've done to impress a girl?
"When I'd saved up enough money I took a girlfriend to a nice hotel for the weekend. We had room service all day long!"

Have you ever met a star you'd previously fancied?
"Yeah, I met Yazz and she's a really gorgeous person."

Do you have a favourite romantic movie that gets you a bit tearful?
"Well, not a movie but the TV programme *thirtysomething*. It was all about relationships and stuff and it was really sad sometimes. The music was good too!"

Which appearance or roadshow stands out as the best for you?
"I'd say the signing in HMV at Oxford Street. The whole street had to be cordoned off by the police for half an hour — oops!"

Tell us what would happen on your ideal date...
"I'd go skinny-dipping with Ariel from *The Little Mermaid* and whisper sweet nothings in her shell-like!"

TONY DOWDING

Tell us the intimate details of your first date...
"Ooh, my first real date! I can remember being really nervous — we went to London to go shopping but I was well embarrassed 'cos I didn't know what to say to her! At the end of the date she kissed me and I was really chuffed, but the next week she started going out with my mate instead!"

Did you ever fancy a teacher at school?
"Yeah I did, she was called Mrs Godfrey — she didn't know I liked her, but she might find out now! I remember we went on a school trip to France with her and I really liked her then."

What's the most embarrassing thing that's happened to you on a date?
"Once when I was very young I was going out with a girl who had a twin sister. Anyway, loads of us went to the cinema, including the twins, and at the end of the date I went to kiss my girlfriend and ended up snogging the wrong sister — she didn't exactly pull away though! That caused a big row!"

What's the silliest thing you've done to impress a girl?
"Joined Bad Boys Inc!"

Have you ever met a star you've previously fancied?
"Not yet — I'm still waiting to meet Lisa Stansfield. I've met Dannii Minogue though and I was quite impressed with her!"

Which romantic movie is guaranteed to turn you into a sobbing wreck?
"*Ghost* — Demi Moore is so sexy!"

Do you have a favourite memory from a public appearance or roadshow?
"I enjoyed the appearance at HMV in London's Oxford Street and we played a club in Bromley which was great fun!"

Describe your ideal date...
"Well, I'm actually quite shy when it comes to asking girls out, so I would like the girl to ask me out first! We'd start off by going to a bar then we'd head off to a club — we'd dance away until about six a.m. then she'd invite me back to her place for a cup of tea! I haven't met my ideal girl yet, but I'm still looking!"

MATTHEW PATEMAN

Tell us the intimate details of your first date, Matthew . . .
"I was 14 and I was at the cinema watching *Rocky IV* with my mate and I was sitting next to this girl who was quite nice. My mate told me to go for it and eventually I plucked up the courage to ask her out!"

Did you ever fancy a teacher at your school?
"Ooh yeah, I really fancied a teacher called Miss Roxburgh. Me and my mate used to sit at the front of the class and giggle at her, she used to go red with embarrassment! She was nice though."

What's the most embarrassing thing that's happened to you on a date?
"I forgot my money too! I went for a meal with this girl and in the rush to get ready I forgot my wallet, so she had to pay. That was pretty embarrassing."

Have you ever had your heart broken?
"Yeah, a couple of times and I've broken a couple of hearts myself, I think. I still keep in touch with just about everyone I've went out with. I've got all their numbers in a big black book!"

What's the most extravagant thing you've done to impress a girl?
"Erm, nothing really extravagant springs to mind, but I've often bought flowers and chocolates for girlfriends, the usual stuff!"

Have you ever met a star you've previously fancied?
"Well, I thought Kim Wilde was gorgeous too — we all liked her, it seems! I'd really love to meet Madonna and Christy Turlington too!"

Do you have a fave romantic film which is guaranteed to make you cry?
"I really cried when I saw *Beaches*, and I remember crying at *E.T.* because my brother wouldn't stop laughing at me! When I went to see *Ghost* I burst out laughing because this girl in the cinema was really crying, but by the end of the film I was sobbing too!"

Do you have a favourite memory from a P.A.?
"Yeah, I really enjoyed the Newcastle one. We were only expecting about five hundred people there, but we appeared on *Gimme 5* in Newcastle earlier that day and five thousand turned up! There was hardly any security there so it got a bit mad!"

Describe your ideal date . . .
"It would have to be partying in New York with Madonna. We would go clubbing all night — I'm sure she'd know all the best places! We'd have an absolutely wild time."

ALLY BEGG

Do you fancy telling us all about your first date, Ally?
"It was when I was 13 — I went to the cinema with a girl called Laura. We had a great time and I gave her a sloppy snog before she got her bus home!"

Did you ever fancy one of your school teachers?
"Nah — they were all too old and grumpy!"

What's the most embarrassing thing that's happened to you on a date?
"Nothing really — I should count my lucky stars I suppose!"

Have you ever had your heart broken?
"Only once, by a girl called Pauline. I was madly in love with her and she dumped me for another man! The night she dumped me I got a bit drunk and severely regretted it the next morning."

What's the silliest thing you've done to impress a girl?
"Nothing — I've never tried to impress a girl just in case I make a complete prat of myself!"

Have you ever met a star you've previously fancied?
"Ooh yeah — I met Kim Wilde at the Capitol F.M. Concert at Crystal Palace and I was completely blown away! She is so sexy!"

Do you have a favourite romantic film you're guaranteed to sob at?
"Well, I love *Ghost* but I don't really cry at films."

At which public appearance or roadshow did you receive the best response?
"I'd have to say the one in Newcastle which was completely mad! Over five thousand kids turned up — they mobbed our car and totally wrecked it! It was also my 21st birthday that day so that made it that little bit special."

Describe your ideal date . . .
"It would be with Kim Wilde again — I would take her to a desert island and give her the time of her life!"

battle of the bands

Does every girl in the land still love **Take That** or are people coming round to the other **boy bands** on the scene? We took to the streets to find out . . .

LINDSAY WALLACE (13)
"**Take That** are brilliant, because they're so gorgeous. They started out being the best dancers, and all these other bands have tried to copy them. None of the others are any good."

LYNN MILLER (13)
"I don't listen to anything apart from my **Take That** records. They're the best band in the world — my favourite single is *Could It Be Magic?* and my favourite man is Mark Owen!"

LAURA PRATT (13)
"I've loved **Take That** for ages, mainly because I really fancy Robbie. I think **East 17** are ugly, and they can't sing!"

LEANNE BECMAN (13)
"I prefer **Take That** to **East 17**, because **East 17** just think they're so cool. All of **Take That** are hunky and sexy, and they bring out great singles!"

LISA TAYLOR (13)
"I like **East 17** the best. I think **Take That** are a bunch of saps, and none of them can compare to Terry — he's definitely the best looking guy. As for all the other male bands that seem to have suddenly appeared . . . they're just copy cats, and don't have any real talent. None of them could put out a single like *House of Love* — it's a classic!"

DEBBIE URE (15)
"I'm so glad you've asked me, because I've got a claim to fame! I've met **Take That**!! My friend won a competition to go for a day out with the band, and I got to go, too! They were really nice, and dead easy to get on with, as well as being gorgeous! So, not surprisingly, **Take That** are easily my favourite band."

LISA MURRAY (13)
"You shouldn't even have to ask who the best band are — I love Mark Owen, so I think **Take That** are brilliant!"

LOUISE GLOVER (13)
"I love **East 17** the best, because they've got a bit of a rough image! Those bands that try to make out they're all goody-goody are really false — at least **East 17** don't pretend to be something they're not!"

CINDY REEKIE (15)
"I love **Take That**, because they've got everything! They're good-looking, I love their singles, and their dance routines are really impressive. Some of the other male bands are quite talented, too, but they don't come anywhere near **Take That**."

LISA KING (15)
"**Take That** are brilliant! They're gorgeous and have loads of great songs. The other bands all try to copy them, but they're useless, especially **East 17** — they can't sing to save themselves!"

CLAIRE McGREGOR (15)
"I know I'm the odd one out here, but I don't like any of these stupid, girly bands — all the guys in them think they're real babes! If I like a song, it doesn't matter who it's by."

YVONNE MACDONALD (15)
"I love **Take That** — I really fancy them! **East 17** are a bunch of no-hopers. They're ugly, they can't sing, their dancing is rubbish and I hate their attitude. They'll never have a single as good as *Pray*!"

SUZANNE WRIGHT (13)
'I love **Take That**, because I love Robbie and Mark!'

CASEY BALD (14)
"**Take That** are the best of all the bands that are around, because they produce the best music, and they're gorgeous! But I think that all these bands that are around are just copying **New Kids On The Block** — remember them? I loved them when they were big."

GAIL MORGAN (14)
"I like **Take That** and **Bad Boys Inc.**, because they've both got nice-looking guys in them. I think the reason that all these boy bands have been appearing is because they appeal to young girls because of their looks mainly, although the music's pretty good too. Unfortunately, **East 17** are ugly!"

KERRY HALLEY (14)
"I like **Take That**, and I loved *A Million Love Songs*. I can see the appeal of bands like **Worlds Apart** and **Bad Boys**, as well, because they've got really good-looking guys in them, too."

LOUISE PEEBLES (14)
"I like **Take That**, mainly for their looks, but the music's pretty good, too! It's weird, because I hated them when they first came out. They seemed to be on TV all the time, in every magazine, but they never had a hit single. I remember thinking that they should just give up as they were obviously useless! I've changed my mind now, though, because the singles they're putting out now are good."

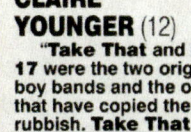

LESLEY HASTIE (16)
"I like **Take That** the best, and I know a lot of people will shout me down for this, but my favourite lad is Howard — his body's brilliant, and he looks really fit. Their music's okay, but I'll admit they're not the most original band around as far as singles go — it's looks that do it for me, though."

YVONNE LLEWELLYN (17)
"I listen to all types of music and don't feel you can only like one band and you've to stick with them forever. I'll go for anything! I will admit to fancying Mark Owen, though!"

ELAINE PATERSON (17)
"I think **Take That**'s singles are good, but the lads in **Worlds Apart** are much nicer-looking. I don't know their names, but I always fancy the whole group whenever I see them in things. The only thing I don't like about **Worlds Apart** is that they don't seem to be able to put out an original single — they always do cover versions. But I really liked *Everlasting Love*."

LAURA CURRAN (14)
"There seem to be loads of boy bands around and my favourite is **East 17** — other bands are just like little kids compared to them. **East 17** have a harder edge, and don't waste time trying to be clean cut. Apart from that, they've got real talent — the only talent **Take That** have is that they can all jump about on stage at the same time. Big deal . . ."

JACKIE WRIGHT (15)
"**Take That** are brilliant, and I wish I could meet Robbie because I fancy him, but I think their songs are great, too. I don't mind **East 17** either, although I know girls don't like you to like **Take That** and **East 17**. **East 17** are more original and don't just have the usual poppy, chart numbers — but I don't fancy any of them!"

CLAIRE YOUNGER (12)
"**Take That** and **East 17** were the two original boy bands and the ones that have copied them are rubbish. **Take That** are the best, with **East 17** a long way behind them. My favourite single is *Pray* and I'm madly in love with Robbie — he's so good-looking."

CHARLENE CUNNINGHAM (13)
"I like **Take That**, because they're all so nice-looking. All these other bands are just copy-cats, and to be honest, it's difficult to tell them apart. **Bad Boys Inc.**, **Worlds Apart**, **Let Loose** . . . what's the difference? They're all just trying to jump on the bandwagon."

Well, judging by most of the answers, **Take That** still seem to be the most popular band around, partly due to their looks and partly because of their talent! **East 17** are a bit further behind, and **Bad Boys Inc** seem to be the most popular 'copy-cat' band. Why not let us know what you think? We want to hear about which band you like, so you can drop us a line to **Battle Of The Bands**, *Shout* Magazine, P.O. Box 305, London NW1 1TX.

"We've got more to offer than Take That!"

Are you surprised by the success you've had this year?
TONY — "Not really. We worked hard to get to this point in our careers and I think the songs are good — we've got a lot to offer. We're part of the future of music unlike Take That, whose act is still rooted in the 70's. I'm not knocking them because they work really hard and their stage routine is much more together than ours but musically we've got far more to offer. I don't think they'll be around in a few years but we will."

Have you earned lots of money this year?
JOHN — "If we have, we haven't seen it yet!"
TONY — "Most of this year has been spent paying off our debt to the record company. It cost us £350,000 to make the album and promote it and stuff. We've just about paid that off so everything we make from now on will be profit."

What'll you buy with the first sign of profits?
TONY — "I'd like to buy a good studio for recording — something we can always use."

off steam. It was part of growing up. At the time I just thought it was a laugh, but now I'd hate anyone to nick my car or stereo."
TONY — "Yeah. I'm bored by all that now. I feel like I've been there, done that. I want new experiences."

Do you feel more responsible now?
JOHN — "We have to be careful what we do because we're in the spotlight. We used to be pretty wild, but we've calmed down as we were presenting a bad image. We still like to relax with a few beers, though!"

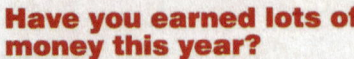
They're not keen on Take That! They don't like the Pet Shop Boys! *Shout* gets bitchy with East 17!

Have you finished the new album?
TONY — "Yeah, I've written it all at home in my makeshift studio but we haven't started recording it yet. It's gonna be a complete change from *Walthamstow* — less rap, more songs. We don't want to be pigeon-holed as white rappers, we're more versatile."

The Pet Shop Boys didn't really like your version of *West End Girls*, did they?
TONY — "Er, I think it was 50-50. I don't care though. We don't like them anyway. We only did it because our manager, Tom Watkins, said it would be a good idea and he's their manager too!"

TERRY — "I'd like to get a nice flat, pay it off straight away so you're not worried about mortgages or anything."
JOHN — "Yeah, same here. A studio like this (looks around the snoot photographer's studio) would be nice."

Tony, has your baby daughter Atlanta changed your view of the world?
TONY — "Yeah, I suppose it has. It's given me more drive and ambition. I want to do well so I can provide for her. Although I'm still not used to getting up in the middle of the night each time she starts crying and I'm not very good at nappy-changing!"

Why do you reckon you got into so much trouble when you were younger?
JOHN — "For us, joyriding and stuff was just a way of having fun and letting

Did you enjoy school?
TONY — "Schooldays definitely weren't the happiest days of my life and I think a lot of teenagers would agree with me. There are just so many problems to cope with nowadays and I think there's too much discipline in schools.
"It's really important to learn the basics, but school doesn't prepare you for later life. No way."

Any plans for a well-earned break?
TONY — "We've had our one and only holiday this year. Me, John and Terry went to Hawaii and it was brilliant. My family could never afford holidays when I was younger, so it was the first time I'd had one abroad.
"We even tried canoeing! I got a bit panicky when it overturned though — I thought I was going to drown or be eaten by a shark!"

Shout bumped into the lads from Boyzone at Atlantic 252 for a quick gossip!

BOYZ TALK!

Who gets on your nerves?
★Steve: "People who smoke. It's disgusting and I'd never go out with a girl who smoked."
★Shane: "I hate people who try to put us down. Some interviewers are really sarcastic and say things like 'So are you really big-headed now?' That does my head in."
★Ronan: "I can't stand liars. They're really sad."
★Mikey: "People who ask nosey questions!"
★Keith: "Anyone who's greedy."

What false names do you use to check into hotels?
★Steve: "Mostly we just use our real first names and different surnames of people we know."
★Keith: "I went through a stage of checking in as Tom Cruise!"

Who's the messiest when you're on tour?
★Shane: "Ronan's really messy. He throws his clothes everywhere."
★Mikey: "None of us are tidy, apart from Steve. We're usually so tired that we don't have time to clean up behind us."

What's the nicest country you've visited?
★Shane: "Everywhere we go has its good points — it'd be hard to choose a favourite. We don't get to see much of the places we visit cos we're either in hotels or busy with interviews and appearances."

What would you do if you won the lottery?
★Ronan: "I'd buy a house and a car, give some money to charity and make sure my family were well looked after."
★Keith: "I'd like to go on a Caribbean cruise."
★Shane: "I don't do the lottery. I'd rather someone worse off than me won the jackpot."

What do you do to relax?
★Steve: "I love chilling out and watching a video whenever I get the chance."
★Keith: "I go swimming. It's really relaxing."
★Mikey: "I'm trying to get into meditation."

What's your favourite chocolate bar?
★Ronan: "I love Galaxy — it's the nicest chocolate ever."
★Shane: "I don't eat chocolate. I gave it up when I was sixteen and started going to the gym."

Which film would you have liked to star in?
★Shane: "Bad Boys. Will Smith's character is so cool."
★Keith: "Point Break."
★Ronan: "Batman. He's my hero!"

What ambitions do you still have?
★Ronan: "At some point in the future I'd like to settle down and have a family."
★Keith: "I'd love Boyzone to do well in America."
★Mikey: "To become more rich and more famous!"

"NONE OF US ARE TIDY!"

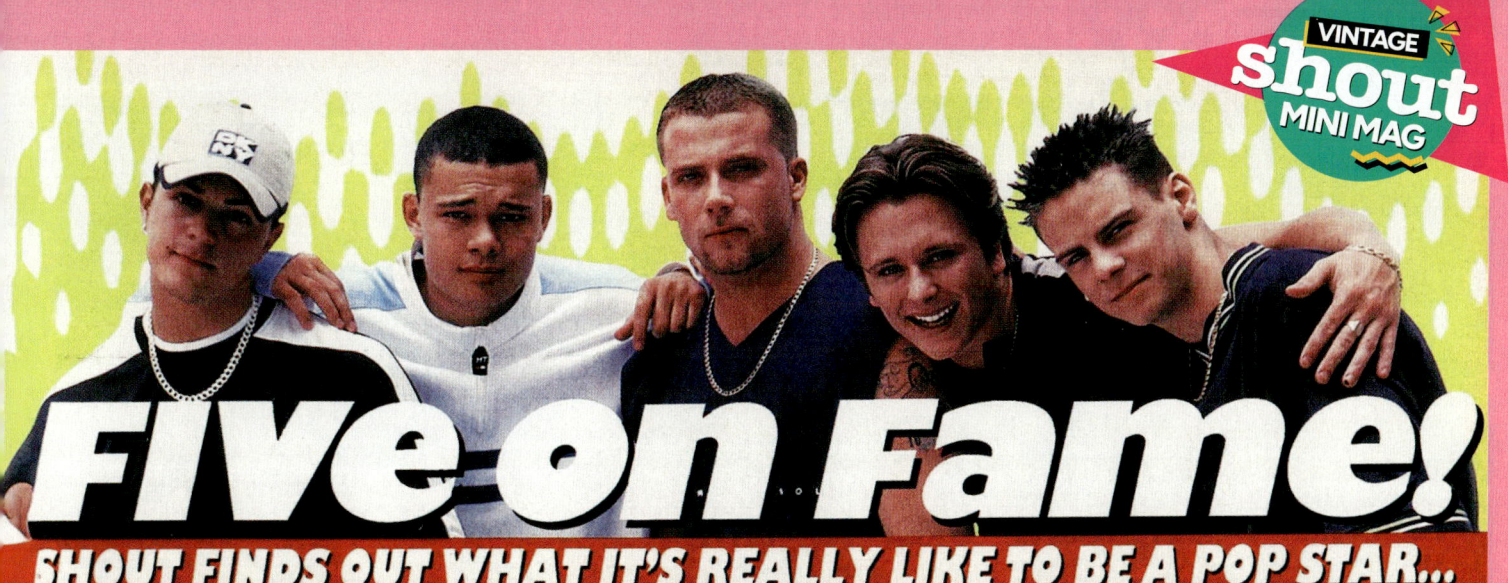

Five on Fame!
SHOUT FINDS OUT WHAT IT'S REALLY LIKE TO BE A POP STAR...

★ IS BEING FAMOUS AS MUCH FUN AS IT LOOKS?
SCOTT: "No! Obviously we have a laugh but people don't see how hard it is. I think we work harder than any other band."
J: "In the beginning it was all fun, but then it started to get tough. We began to think 'Is it worth it?', but it's chilled out a bit now. We usually have a good time but we're not false — if we're having a bad time, you'll see it as well."

★ DO YOU GET FED UP WITH FAME?
RICH: "Yeah, there are times when I throw a pop star tantrum, especially when I'm tired. I'm okay when I wake up the next day, though."
SCOTT: "It gets me down when we're not getting enough sleep and missing meals. When I feel like that, I try to think of all the brilliant things about being in Five."
SEAN: "There's times when I get stressed out, like when we have to do the same things every day. It gets a bit boring. Sometimes we really need a break."

★ HOW HAVE YOUR LIVES CHANGED OVER THE PAST YEAR?
ABS: "My life's changed in a huge way. Before Five, I was at home or at college. Now in a fortnight I could be in Japan, come home, appear on TV, go to America, sing in front of ten thousand people...it's amazing!"
SCOTT: "Our lives have changed, but we've not changed as people. I'm still the same person I was before and I don't act like a big pop star or look down on my old mates."
J: "We get invited to big showbiz parties now but to be honest I'd rather go home and hang out with my friends."

★ DO YOU HAVE TIME FOR GIRLFRIENDS?
SCOTT: "I really want a girlfriend, but there's no time!"
J: "I've met girls I could have fallen in love with, but there's no time. We've met nice girls all over the world, but there's no way I could have a serious girlfriend. I can't even remember the last time I kissed a girl!"
RICH: "I don't have a girlfriend, but one newspaper said I was going out with Lisa from Steps. I'd only talked to her at a party! I'd like to meet someone, but we're never in the same place for long."
SEAN: "I fell in love a year ago, but we broke up when I joined Five. I still talk to her as a friend."
ABS: "I've been going out with Danielle for two years. We know we're going to be away from each other a lot, but we've learned to deal with it. The other guys don't know if girls they meet now only like them cos they're in Five."

★ WHAT ARE YOUR AMBITIONS FOR THIS YEAR?
SCOTT: "I want Five to be the biggest band, and we'll have to work hard to achieve it."
RICH: "I'd like a number one single and a decent night's sleep!"
ABS: "All I want is for Five to stay together and be successful."

★ DO YOU MISS YOUR PRIVACY?
SCOTT: "I love the fact that fans want my autograph, but sometimes I'm tired. Our fans should avoid me late at night!"

★ DO YOU THINK YOU'D BE FRIENDS IF YOU WEREN'T IN FIVE?
J: "At first I thought I wouldn't get on with Abs or Sean, but now I think they're great. One thing we have in common is that we all have a messed-up sense of humour!"

> "we've not changed as people."

> "we get invited to big showbiz parties."

VINTAGE shout MINI MAG

The guys chat with Zoe Ball.

Shout got up early to spend a morning with Boyzone at top TV show Fully Booked. Read on for all the fun.

Always time to sign an autograph!

Time for another song...

...and it's a real smoochy one to finish off with!

BACKSTREET CHAT!
BOY TALK WITH THE HUNKY BSB.

Is it true that there's going to be a Backstreet Boys movie?
Kev: "We've been offered lots of movies and scripts but we really want to focus on music right now. Music will always come first for us."
Howie: "We like to keep people surprised though, so you'll just have to wait and see what happens."

What do you think of other boy bands?
Kev: "There are so many boy bands out there that it's like looking in a mirror every time a new one comes up. It's flattering when people imitate us and we try to take it as a compliment, but it's really important for us to keep ahead of the game."

"We're trying to write our own songs."

AJ: "I think *Everybody (Backstreet's Back)* was a turning point for us. It made a statement that we can stand on our own and that we're different from other boy bands out there."

Are any of you thinking about going solo?
Brian: "We're working on our own material more and more but it's for the group. We're trying to write our own songs for Backstreet Boys."

"It's flattering when people imitate us."

Howie: "Yeah, solo albums don't come into it yet. Maybe in the future, if we feel like taking a break from the group, we might go solo. I think we still have a long way to go with Backstreet Boys first."

How long do you think BSB will last?
Kev: "Until we stop enjoying it. When the fun stops, so do we."
AJ: "We'll keep going as long as our music lasts in people's hearts."

How do you cope with fans following you?
Kev: "It's really amazing — they know what we're up to before we even do!"
AJ: "The fans are very smart at tracking us down. If we had more time we'd be much better at playing hide 'n' seek with them!"
Nick: "It's got to the stage where we have to take security guys wherever we go. We've got a guard each now."

Do you worry about your fans?
Kev: "We look out for them, especially at concerts. We'd hate any girls to collapse at our shows

"I think we still have a long way to go with Backstreet Boys."

and we try to make sure they're careful."

How do you all get on with Nick's little brother, Aaron?
Kev: "He's a great kid. In Germany we knew he'd arrived in town when we got out of the hotel lift and Aaron was running down the hall screaming 'Nick! Nick!'."
Nick: "Aaron's doing really well and I'm proud of him. My whole family love to entertain and perform so maybe one day my sisters will be famous, too. Anything can happen with my family!"

"Aaron's doing really well."

What are you doing at Christmas?
AJ: "We're actually taking our first proper holiday around Christmas. We're going to have a break with our families and relax."
Brian: "We've only had a few days off this year so it's going to be really nice to chill out at home."

"The fans are very smart at tracking us down."

PARTY PEOPLE

Have you ever played Spin The Bottle?

L "We play it all the time. Spike and Jimmy taught me how it works, and in their version you get asked loads of saucy questions! We don't play the one where you snog girls cos it's usually just the three of us!"

J "We've played Strip Poker a few times. I hate it cos I'm always the one who ends up in my pants!"

S "The only party games I like are Pass The Parcel and Musical Chairs!"

Which songs make you want to dance?

S "Anything dancey that I can really get down to. I like most of the songs in the charts."

L "My top party tunes are Take That's *Relight My Fire* and *Mysterious Girl* by Peter Andre. If I was dancing with a girl I'd ask the DJ to play *Again* by Janet Jackson. It's really slow and slushy — good for snogging to!"

J "I'd dance to anything but if I was with a girl I'd choose *Forever Love* by Gary Barlow."

Who would you least like to turn up at your party?

L "Chris Evans. I don't like him cos he's always going on about how rich he is. He never stops to think about people who aren't as lucky as him."

J "I hate people who're big-headed and full of themselves. No-one like that would get on my yacht."

S "I wouldn't like any of my old teachers to turn up. They all said I'd never make it, but now they've got 911 posters all over the school and boast that I was a pupil there!"

Are you party animals?

L "I'm actually quite shy at parties, but my courage builds up as the night goes on. I'm usually up dancing near the end."

J "I'm definitely a party animal. I love chatting to everyone and going mad on the dancefloor."

S "Me too — parties are for having fun!"

Which girl would you take to your party?

S "The actress **Sharon Stone**. She's gorgeous and I like older women."

L "I wouldn't take a date cos I hope I'd meet a gorgeous girl at the party. I'd just go with Jimmy, Spike and my best mate, Potty(!)."

J "**Louise**, cos everyone would be dead impressed. I think she's lovely."

911's fab new single Party People is out this month.

Find out the facts on East 17's Tony and Terry...
eastenders

Terry Coldwell was born on the 24th of July, 1974 — he'll be 19 in a few weeks!

TERRY COLDWELL

- The first record he bought was a rap record by Whistle called *(Nothing Serious) Just Buggin'* in 1986.
- Like Tony, the highlights of Terry's career so far are signing his record deal and appearing on *Top Of The Pops*.
- His fave characters in soapland are the rough, tough and balding Mitchell brothers in *EastEnders*.
- Top tunes of the last few months, according to Terry are rap records *Jump Around* by House Of Pain and *Hip Hop Hooray* by Naughty By Nature.
- He's got a massive crush on Michelle Pfeiffer and Mariah Carey.
- Terry's favourite place out of all his East 17 travels is Hamburg.
- He's got a massive hat collection and at the last count had over 60!
- Terry's the champion computer game player in East 17, although they're all pretty addicted.
- According to Terry, who gets the most fan mail in the band? Levi!
- When asked who was the worst dressed person in the world, Terry answered "Noel Edmonds"!
- The rest of the band all say that Terry is the laziest bloke in the band, and he admits it!
- Despite his ruff, tuff image, Terry has a sensitive side! He admits the last time he cried was when his dog died. Sniff!

Tony was born on the 21st of October, 1970.

TONY MORTIMER

- The first single he bought was *Heart Of Glass* by Blondie — a bit trendier than Brian's, which was *Roland Rat Superstar*!
- So far the highlight of his career was signing East 17's record deal with London Records.
- The first pin-up he ever had on his wall was Spiderman!
- Tony's favourite person in the soap world is Rebekah Elmaloglou.
- His favourite song of the past few years is Bobby Brown's *Humpin' Around*.
- Most fanciable girl in the world according to Tone? Sarah Hollis, whoever she is — lucky girl!
- Tony's travelled all over now, but the place that's made the biggest impression is Israel. He says "It was just so amazing!"
- At the moment most of the travelling Tony's doing is linked with work, but the group managed to head for Hawaii recently. And who would be Tony's ideal holiday companion? His cat!
- When asked for a secret about another bloke in the band, Tony replied, "Brian can't dance!"
- What's the strangest fan letter he's ever received? "Once, someone wrote and said they wanted to do unmentionable things to me with jam! If that girl is reading this, hurry up with the jam . . . I'm still waiting!"
- Worst dressed person on the planet, according to Ant? Julian Clary!
- His most-used (printable!) words are Wicked or Blindin'!

GOSSIP

My... New Haircut By Backstreet Boys' Nick

"It wasn't my idea — it was my sister's! She's a hairdresser so she cut it for me and made it blonder by adding a few highlights. I like it, but I think I'll let it grow a bit longer again."

DON'T FORGET...

...to send birthday greetings to Robbie Williams — he's 23 on the 13th...

...this is your last chance to register for the 1997 World Vision 24 Hour Famine which takes place on the 28th. For more info, call the hotline on 0990 24 24 24...

...to listen out for *Indestructible*, the fab new single from Alisha's Attic.

BARLOW GOES BANANAS!

Shout bumped into Gary Barlow and he gave us the recipe for his favourite treat, Banoffi Pie.

You'll need:
- 1 packet of digestive biscuits
- 2 ounces of butter
- 1 tin of condensed milk
- 1/4 pint of double cream
- 2 bananas
- 1 chocolate flake

Smash the whole packet of biscuits with a rolling pin until they're really crumbly, then melt the butter and stir in the crumbs. Put the mixture in a flan dish and push it down with the back of a spoon to make a biscuit base.

Bring a saucepan of water to the boil and then put in the unopened can of condensed milk. Leave it to simmer for two hours. Then, with an adult's help, open the tin and pour the caramel over the biscuit base.

After this has cooled, cover the caramel with sliced banana, then whip up the double cream and spread it on top. For a fab finishing touch, crumble up the flake and sprinkle it on top. The pie will be ready to eat after two hours in the fridge. Gaz warned us, "once you start eating it, you'll never want to stop!"

CORRR! CORNER

East 17's John teases us with a glimpse of his fab body!

did you know...?

...that Declan Donnelly's fave Spice Girl is Emma? Emma went to school with Dec's girlfriend, *2point4 Children* star Claire Buckfield, and the cheeky lad says that's the only reason he likes her best. Not that he fancies her, you understand...!

Kissing Keith!

★ Boyzone's Keith gave *Shout* the goss on his first ever snog. "It was with a girl called Yvonne when we were babysitting at a friend's house. I was really scared my dad would know I'd been kissing, so I splashed my lips with cold water before I went home!"

Time For Trouble!

If you're looking for TV with a difference, tune into Trouble, the fab new satellite channel which launches on Feb 3. Trouble is jam-packed with all the teen shows you used to enjoy on TCC, from *Heartbreak High* and *Byker Grove* to *California Dreams* and *Saved By The Bell*. Look out for young Ant and Dec in early episodes of the *Grove*. Don't they look sweet...?!

what do they look like?

This issue — 911's Lee Brennan. Wake up!

STAR MAKER

If it wasn't for former journalist Alex Kadis, Take That may never have become the boyband superstars they did

Former journalist Alex

It is early summer 1993. At the central London HQ of best-selling teen music mag *Smash Hits*, features editor Alex Kadis is pitching an unusual, never-tried-before idea. That of a fashion shoot with a boyband called Take That.

The five-piece had, to date, enjoyed a modicum of success with singles *It Only Takes a Minute*, *A Million Love Songs* and *Could It Be Magic?* charting in the top ten. But they had yet to make it to the number one spot, become a true pop force to be reckoned with, and household faces and names to boot.

"The editor took some persuading," recalls Alex. "*Smash Hits* didn't do fashion shoots but I knew it would benefit both the band and our magazine. Take That's music was good but at the time, they had this male-stripper 'bare-chests-and-leather-posing-pouches' vibe. Not right for our readership.

"They were all very good-looking so, I figured, why not put them in some great clothes – and onto the cover of *Smash Hits*? The tagline would be, 'Take That as you've never seen them before'.

"We were desperate for a massive new pop act to feature. So, we headed off to a beach in East Sussex which doubled for California and photographed the boys. It was a great success.

"I took to the five of them – Gary, Robbie, Mark, Howard and Jason – from the off. They were funny, down-to-earth and very endearing. Just really nice lads."

It's no exaggeration to say it was that *Smash Hits* cover – and therefore Alex's original idea – that sent Take That soaring into the superstardom stratosphere.

In July 1993 – just a few weeks after featuring in the pop mag – the band achieved their first UK number one single with *Pray*, followed over the next few years by a host of pop hits.

Alex became so close to the band that their manager Nigel Martin-Smith offered her a job. She was to oversee the running of their fan club in addition to starting a Take That magazine and putting together a book about the band called *Take That in Private* with photographer Philip Ollerenshaw.

The book gave fans an intimate glimpse into the lives of Gary, Howard, Jason, Mark and Robbie, showcasing behind-the-scenes moments that highlighted their personalities beyond the stage. All this entailed Alex going on several world tours with the band.

"It was quite crazy," she recalls. "The itinerary was relentless for the boys. Plus, the more famous they became, the more people wanted a part of them and were desperate to get close to them.

"There would be fans climbing up drainpipes of hotels in an attempt to get in. Fans sneaking along hotel corridors and landings to find the guys' rooms. In the end, I insisted on a room on a different floor so I wouldn't keep being woken up.

"There was one occasion in Italy when it felt like our lives were at risk due to

> **It was reported that it was massive rivalry between Robbie and Gary that caused Robbie to start drinking to excess but I recall it being more about the overwhelming pressure of being in Take That**

manic fans. After a gig, we'd left the venue in the tour bus, only to be followed by what seemed like a fleet Vespas ridden by fans. They kept dodging in front of us, trying to get the bus to stop. It was really dangerous but eventually we managed to shake them off."

What was Alex's relationship like with the boys on a personal level? A bit like a big sister?

"More like friends," she replies. "Professional friends. I liked them both individually and as a unit. They genuinely loved each other, you know.

"The fractures only started when Robbie started going off the rails in late 1994.

"It was reported it was

Their early style definitely turned heads!

Alex says the band were just "really nice lads"

'HIDING' ROBBIE

When Robbie Williams left Take That in July 1995, he was desperate for some down time.

"He wanted to go somewhere he wouldn't be recognised," Alex remembers. "I was going to a little place in Turkey called Kalkan where my sister was living. Back then, it was very quiet and I suggested Robbie come, too.

"He agreed but within hours of us getting there, he'd spotted a magazine with Take That on the cover. He bought a copy and walked around with it held up to his face. 'This is me,' he kept saying to anyone we passed. It made me laugh. He'd said he wanted anonymity. He didn't really!"

Avoiding the limelight!

massive rivalry between Robbie and Gary that caused Robbie to start drinking to excess but I recall it being more about the overwhelming pressure of being in Take That.

"Robbie had only been 15 when he joined the band. It was always clear from the start that Gary was the songwriter.

"Their manager had put Take That together in the first place as a kind of support group for Gary. Things became more equal when it became apparent that the other four members – and especially Mark and Robbie – were very appealing to their young fans.

"Personally, I probably got along with Jason the best. He was a bit older than the others and so closer in age to me. We spent a lot of time together – but only on a platonic basis may I add!"

After the band split in 1996 – Robbie having exited the year before – Alex went on to manage Mark as a solo artist for several years. When Take That reformed in 2005, they wanted her to work for them again.

"I said, 'Thanks but no thanks'," she explains. "I was in my 40s by then and working for Sony Records. Going back to working with Take That – much as I'd loved it in the 90s – would have felt like going backwards."

Now 63, Alex who lives in East London, works as a music manager and consultant, and co-hosts the podcast *Poptastic* in which she chats about all things pop with a former *Smash Hits* colleague. She has also returned to her writing roots. Her first novel *Big Nobody* is published by Penguin Random House next February.

Apart from the occasional catch-up with Mark, she's no longer in contact with the Take That boys.

"Not because of any falling out. It's what happens with work friends, isn't it? You move on when you stop working together.

"When I look back now, I realise how lucky I was to be involved with Take That in their glory days. It was a fabulous, crazy time – and I doubt we'll see its like again."

GUESS THE LYRIC!

1 "You are my fire, the one desire"

2 "You're all I ever wanted, you're all I ever needed, yeah"

3 "You have so many relationships in this life, only one or two will last"

4 "Girl, you know we belong together, I have no time for you to be playin' with my heart like this"

5 "Got a picture of you beside me, got your lipstick mark still on your coffee cup"

6 "I wanna know, who ever told you I was letting go"

7 "Hey girl, in your eyes I see a picture of me all the time"

8 "Baby I really know by now, since we met that day, you showed me the way"

9 "No matter what they tell us, no matter what they do"

10 "Five bad boys with the power to rock you, blowing your mind so you gotta get into"

11 "I don't care who you are, where you're from, what you did, as long as you love me"

12 "It's tearin' up my heart when I'm with you, but when we are apart, I feel it too"

13 "Motownphilly's back again, doin' a little east coast swing"

14 "All I do each night is pray, hoping that I'll be a part of you again someday"

15 "If I let you go, I will never know what my life would be holding you close to me"

16 "You can't see me, I'm the invisible man"

17 "It's only words, and words are all I have to take your heart away"

18 "I'll be there for you until the time is through"

19 "But my love is all I have to give, without you I don't think I can live"

20 "You might've been hurt, babe, that ain't no lie"

21 "Close your eyes, make a wish, and blow out the candlelight"

22 "Girl, you're everything a man could want and more"

23 "So impossible as they may seem, you've got to fight for every dream"

24 "So many words for the broken heart, it's hard to see in a crimson love"

25 "The hardest thing I'll ever have to do is look you in the eye and tell you I don't love you"

Answers: 1 Backstreet Boys - "I Want it That Way", 2 *NSYNC - "Back for Good", 3 Hanson - "MMMBop", 4 Boyz II Men - "End of the Road", 5 Take That - "Back for Good", 6 Westlife - "Swear It Again", 7 New Kids on the Block - "Step by Step", 8 98 Degrees - "Because of You", 9 Boyzone - "No Matter What", 10 Five - "Slam Dunk (Da Funk)", 11 Backstreet Boys - "As Long As You Love Me", 12 *NSYNC - "Tearin' Up My Heart", 13 Boyz II Men - "Motownphilly", 14 Take That - "Pray", 15 Westlife - "If I Let You Go", 16 98 Degrees - "Invisible Man", 17 Boyzone - "Words", 18 Five - "Until the Time is Through", 19 Backstreet Boys - "All I Have to Give", 20 *NSYNC - "It's Gonna Be Me", 21 Boyz II Men - "I'll Make Love to You", 22 Take That - "Everything Changes", 23 Westlife - "Flying Without Wings", 24 Backstreet Boys - "Show Me the Meaning of Being Lonely", 25 98 Degrees - "The Hardest Thing"

MID-LATE 1990s

59

Part two
ULTIMATE
TAKE THAT

Pop perfection and personal chaos – when it came to boyband drama, nobody did it more heartbreakingly than Take That

What's a boyband without a bit of chaos?

> The band carried on winning awards and topping charts as a four-piece

Is a boyband even really a boyband without some major drama thrown in every now and then? Take That certainly brought plenty of it in the mid to late 90s as fans experienced serious highs and lows as they followed their favourite band.

The group were riding high on a wave of success with the release of their third album *Nobody Else* in May 1995 which brought us memorable hits such as *Sure* and *Back For Good*.

However, the euphoria was to be shortlived – major change was just around the corner and in July of that year, fans were left distraught at the shock announcement that Robbie Williams was departing.

It was a event that shook the band and their fans to the core but later that same month, the remaining members made a strong return to the charts with one of their most memorable hits – the iconic *Never Forget*, which also poignantly featured vocals from the much-missed Robbie.

The remaining fab four also covered the Bee Gees' *How Deep Is Your Love?*, released in February 1996 and a major chart success, taking the number one spot in the UK charts for three weeks.

However, it was a bittersweet moment as, despite their continuing success as a foursome, that beautiful cover turned out to be their final number one hit following their break-up announcement on February 13, 1996 – news which was met with heartbreak from their dedicated fanbase.

Hysteria engulfed the teen population who heavily mourned the loss of their favourite boyband.

During the late 1990s, the members pursued solo careers with varying degrees of success. Gary Barlow and Mark Owen released solo albums, while Howard Donald returned to his DJ roots.

Robbie, on the other hand, achieved immense success as a solo artist, releasing several hit albums and singles. *Life Thru A Lens*, his debut solo album, was released in 1997 and featured *Angels* – one of the defining anthems from this era. ▶▶

> Going solo – Robbie Williams followed his own path

DID YOU KNOW?
The opening for hit No.1 *Never Forget*, written by Gary Barlow, features a sample from Verdi's Requiem.

TAKE THAT TOP 10

- Back for Good (1995)
- Never Forget (1995)
- How Deep Is Your Love? (1996)
- Patience (2006)
- Shine (2007)
- Rule The World (2007)
- Greatest Day (2008)
- The Flood (2010)
- These Days (2014)
- Giants (2017)

ICONIC

1995
ALBUM SUCCESS
The release of *Nobody Else* in May 1995 was Take That's third studio album, and shot straight to number 1 in the album charts after selling 163,339 copies in its first week alone.

1995
ROBBIE'S DEPARTURE
Robbie Williams left the band in July 1995 sparking a media frenzy as speculation mounted as to what had led to the split.

1996
THEIR FINAL PERFORMANCE
On February 13, 1996, on the Ivo Niehe Show on Dutch TV, the band performed to a small audience of just 250 people.

1996
BREAK-UP
Take That embarked on their final tour as a quartet and then announced their disbandment on February 13, 1996 – a truly heartbreaking moment for fans. More than 200,000 grieving fans contacted a television helpline on ITV's *This Morning*. The Samaritans and Childline set up dedicated phonelines to provide support to distraught teens and some heartbroken teenagers even set up a 'shrine' with

Announcing the split – and breaking teenage hearts – in February 1996

Back for good? The band returned — as a foursome — for a tour in 2006

MOMENTS

posters, flowers and candles outside HMV record store in Oxford Street, London.

1996
HOW DEEP IS YOUR LOVE?
Their cover of the Bee Gees' classic, released on February 26, 1996, became their final number one hit. It remained at the number one spot for three weeks.

LATE 1990S
SOLO VENTURES
Members pursued solo careers, with Robbie Williams achieving notable success with hits like *Angels* and *Millennium*. Gary Barlow's first solo album *Open Road* reached number one in the album charts in 1997 and Mark Owen's first album *Green Man* released in 1996 featured the song *Child* which reached number 3 in the UK charts.

2006 ONWARDS
REUNION
Take That reunited, minus Robbie, for their Ultimate Tour in 2006. It was a massive success and heralded the triumphant return of one of the UK's best loved boybands. In 2010, fans were jubilant, as Robbie joined the rest for their 2010 album *Progress*.

Robbie carried on scoring hits as a solo artist

SMASH HIT SUCCESS

The band at the Brits in 1996

MTV EUROPE MUSIC AWARDS
The band received accolades for their music videos and performances, including Best Live Act in 1995.

BRIT AWARDS
Take That won multiple Brit Awards, including Best British Single for *Back for Good* in 1996.

IVOR NOVELLO AWARDS
Gary Barlow was recognised for his songwriting, winning awards for his contributions to Take That's music, including Most Performed Work for *Back for Good* in 1996.

MTV EUROPE MUSIC AWARDS
Robbie Wiliams's solo career was flying high following the break-up and in 1998 he won Best Solo Artist.

BRIT AWARDS
Robbie Williams mania had firmly taken hold by the end of the decade and in 1999 he won lots of Brit awards including Best British Male Solo Artist, Best British Single for *Angels* and Best British Video for *Millennium*.

DID YOU KNOW?
Before joining Take That, the boys had a variety of jobs. Mark worked as a bank clerk and played football semi-professionally, Howard was a car painter and DJ, Jason was a painter and decorator, breakdancer Gary was performing his music in local clubs... and Robbie hadn't even left school!

DID YOU KNOW?

Behind the frosted tips and chart-topping hits lie some fun facts that you may not know!

Before making it big, Boyzone's line-up looked a little different to what we know today. Two members, Mark Walton and Richard Rock, were replaced by Mikey Graham in a move which left their bandmates reeling at first!

Before Boyz II Men there was Unique Attraction, the name the band went by in their early days. When the band switched to Boyz II Men – a name inspired by a New Edition song – they weren't entirely sold on their new moniker but couldn't think of anything better, so it stuck!

Unlike other bands of the era, the Backstreet Boys never officially split up! Although Kevin Richardson left the band from 2006-2012, the group has continued to tour and record to this very day!

New Kids On The Block fans should mark their calendars! In 1989, the then-governor of the band's home state of Massachusetts declared April 24 'New Kids On The Block Day'. Now, that's a holiday we can get behind!

98 Degrees went against all the traditional trappings of a boyband at the time. Breaking the mould, the group wrote all of their own songs. Notably, they were not formed by a producer, taking a variety of odd jobs to get by until they were signed.

Take That's 2010 album *Progress* became the fastest selling album of the century as 235,000 copies flew off the shelves in just one day! This was the band's sixth studio album and the first to feature the original five-piece since Robbie Williams' exit in 1995.

NSYNC's Lance Bass dreamed of stardom in more ways than one! Lance trained to be a cosmonaut, undergoing extensive mission training in Russia with hopes of going to the International Space Station. Unfortunately, it was not to be as his sponsor for the flight pulled out.

ULTIMATE 911

From a Glasgow flat to global fame, 911 were the pop trio who made the 90s feel like forever

Following 911's split, Jimmy faced challenges with alcohol and drug addiction, leading to a period of depression. He has since recovered and now advocates for mental health support for artists

911 were catchy, cheeky and totally charming

The band, from left, Jimmy, Lee and Spike

DEBUT SINGLE AND ALBUM
The band's first single was called *Night To Remember* and it came out in April 1996. Shortly after followed their debut album *The Journey* which was eventually certified Gold.

Pop favourites 911 formed in 1995 and produced three studio albums and 13 singles until their split in 2000. The group consisted of Lee Brennan, Jimmy Constable and Simon "Spike" Dawbarn.

Jimmy and Spike were dancers who met in the early 1990s. They had both booked gigs on the ITV music show *The Hit Man and Her*, similar to Jason Orange of Take That. After observing that group's success, the pair started their own group together.

Steve Gilmour, who at one point managed Boyzone, met the pair at a radio station, and suggested Lee as the third and final member of the group before agreeing to manage them.

They would then tour around schools and nightclubs in the UK, living from Lee's three-bedroom flat in Glasgow.

CAREER PROGRESSION

Although together for just five years, 911 achieved 10 UK top 10 singles and sold roughly six million albums worldwide. In 1998, their sophomore album *Moving On* came out and was certified Silver, as was *There It Is* when it came out in 1999.

They were eventually signed to Richard Branson's Virgin Records on a £3.5 million deal and were expected to produce four albums, but reached their "peak", according to Dawbarn, in 2000.

Some smash hits from the band included *Don't Make Me Wait*, *Private Number*, *A Little Bit More* and *Bodyshakin'*.

WHAT CAME NEXT?

Just before the band split up in 2000, they released an compilation album called *The Greatest Hits and a Little Bit More*, which included one last single named *Wonderland*.

They later reunited in 2008 in a UK and Irish nightclub tour performing their greatest hits, and again in 2012 when they starred in the documentary series *The Big Reunion*.

The series also starred Atomic Kitten, Liberty X, B*Witched, Five and Honeyz.

In 2013, they also did a comeback performance at London's Hammersmith Apollo, which was sold out.

Back together for *The Big Reunion*

RONAN WHO?

Michelle Barrett's first ever fashion job was a biggie – helping to style boyband megastars Boyzone and Westlife!

Michelle enjoyed being stylist to the stars

Fashion student Michelle Barrett wondered if she'd bitten off more than she could chew. She had jumped at the chance to assist one of the main stylists at a huge weekend event – the Smash Hit Poll Winners Party and Miss World – at London's Olympia in December 1999.

"I can do that," she'd said breezily when a friend who worked in TV had asked her if she knew anyone who could help. "No problem!"

But now she was actually in situ – and in the crazy mayhem that was merely the rehearsals – she wondered if she actually could. And, OMG, had she just put her foot in it! "I'd been rushing around like a mad thing, thinking of a hundred things at once while also trying to find Alex, the stylist I was working for," she recalls. "I finally saw him and rushed up to him – interrupting the conversation he was having with another guy.

"Fortunately, Alex was cool about it and, in fact, introduced me to who he was talking to. 'Michelle – this is Ronan, Ronan – meet Michelle!' I could feel myself blushing. I'd only gone and interrupted Ronan Keating, the biggest Boyzone heartthrob, and one of the biggest acts performing! He was really famous – and I was really embarrassed. He couldn't have been nicer, though.

"Some pop stars might have ignored me or been rude but Ronan was sweetness itself. And continued to be so for the rest of the event. I was very grateful for that.

"It was my first job and I'd been so green.

"Experience working with many big stars since has taught me that first impressions are rarely wrong. And my first impression of Ronan – and, in fact, all the boys in Boyzone and Westlife – was that they were really

> **"You do end up seeing a lot of pop stars in their underpants. It becomes normal, though. That said, I never saw Boyzone or Westlife in theirs!"**

lovely guys. So young, though. Especially Westlife."

That mortifying moment turned into a career-defining one. Michelle went on to dress artists for the Brits, the MOBOs, music videos and international tours, working with acts like Katy Perry and Professor Green. Has she ever been starstruck?

"Not really, to be honest," she replies, "although I did have a bit of a reality check when I found myself dressing Jermaine Jackson at the MOBO awards. The thing is, it's a job and you're so

The Westlife boys always looked sharp

Boyzone's Ronan and Stephen both looked great in a suit!

BOYBAND STYLE – THE LOOKS THAT MADE POP HISTORY

In the early 1990s, Take That set the blueprint for British boyband style – shirtless vests, leather trousers and matching ensembles that screamed peak MTV. As their sound matured, so did their wardrobe – think velvet blazers, tailored coats and a blend of Northern grit and stage glam.

Over in the US, Backstreet Boys and NSYNC brought us oversized cargos, 'shoe-shined' hair and enough coordinated leather to clothe a motorbike gang. Their looks were chaotic but unified and often mirrored their vocals – for instance, tinted sunglasses, matching tracksuits and head-to-toe white for emotional key changes.

Closer to home, Boyzone gave us soft, romantic tailoring while Westlife, in their prime, looked a million dollars in crisp shirts and tailored suits. And who can forget that legendary all-white moment during *Flying Without Wings?* The 2000s saw Blue and Busted mix skinny jeans, military jackets and a dash of pop-punk rebellion, while One Direction made indie-casual the new cool.

Early Take That were 'peak MTV'

Leather-tastic NSYNC!

Boyzone offered 'romantic tailoring'

concentrated on what you have to do, that takes precedence over everything.

"You do end up seeing a lot of pop stars in their underpants. It becomes normal, though. That said, I never saw Boyzone or Westlife in theirs – thankfully! I was just the assistant back then, so I wasn't doing those close-up fittings. As a beginner, I probably would have found it really embarrassing."

These days Michelle runs her own consultancy in Brighton as The Capsule Closet Stylist, helping real people – not pop stars – refine their wardrobes, shop smarter and dress with more confidence.

But does she miss dressing famous folk? "Aspects of it," she replies. "When, for example, you're walking under the tunnel at the O2 with Katy Perry just before she goes on stage… The crowd are screaming, shouting her name and the whole place erupts when she when she walks out… That gives you goosebumps.

"But on the other hand, working with real people is so rewarding because you can make a real difference to their lives. You can absolutely help transform someone who has confidence issues by showing them what to wear."

Back to Ronan Keating – does Michelle rate his style choices today? "He looks great," she smiles, "especially in a sharp suit!"
Capsuleclosetstylist.com

ULTIMATE FIVE

They weren't squeaky clean – and that's why we loved them! Five gave us chaos, charisma and undeniable pop brilliance

DID YOU KNOW?
Five's cover of Queen's *We Will Rock You* featured guest appearances from Queen members Brian May and Roger Taylor.

In the polished world of 90s pop, Five brought spark and swagger

The band were created as a male equivalent to The Spice Girls

We had the squeaky-clean boybands like Boyzone and Westlife in the late 90s then suddenly Five burst on to the scene bringing their infectious bad boy energy and an altogether more rebellious edge that set them apart from the competition.

Formed in 1997, the group consisted of Jason "J" Brown, Abz Love, Scott Robinson, Ritchie Neville, and Sean Conlon. Selected from over 3,000 hopefuls in auditions overseen by Spice Girls managers Bob and Chris Herbert, Five quickly captured the public's attention.

From Ritchie's blue eyes and floppy hair to Abz's sense of mischief, there was something special about all of them and they attracted fans in their thousands.

Signed by Simon Cowell to RCA Records, Five launched their career with the high-energy debut single *Slam Dunk (Da Funk)* in December 1997. Reaching number 10 in the UK Singles Chart, this track set the stage for Five's global success, showcasing their unique blend of rap and catchy pop tunes. The following two years saw them dominate the charts with songs like *When The Lights Go Out*, *If Ya Gettin' Down* and *Everybody Get Up*. In October 1999, they finally reached that coveted number one spot in the charts with *Keep On Movin'*.

Five's music resonated worldwide and they spent the 90s on tour, whipping fans up into a frenzy with their high-energy dance performances on stage. Over 20 million records were sold and they bagged numerous awards. Sadly, global success came at a price and the relentless pressures of fame proved too much for the band to withstand. In 2001, hearts were broken when the news came out that the band members had decided to part ways.

However, fans were thrilled earlier this year when the band announced they were reuniting as a quintet for the first time in 25 years and will tour the UK in autumn 2025.

Scott once owned a memorabilia shop in Leigh-on-Sea

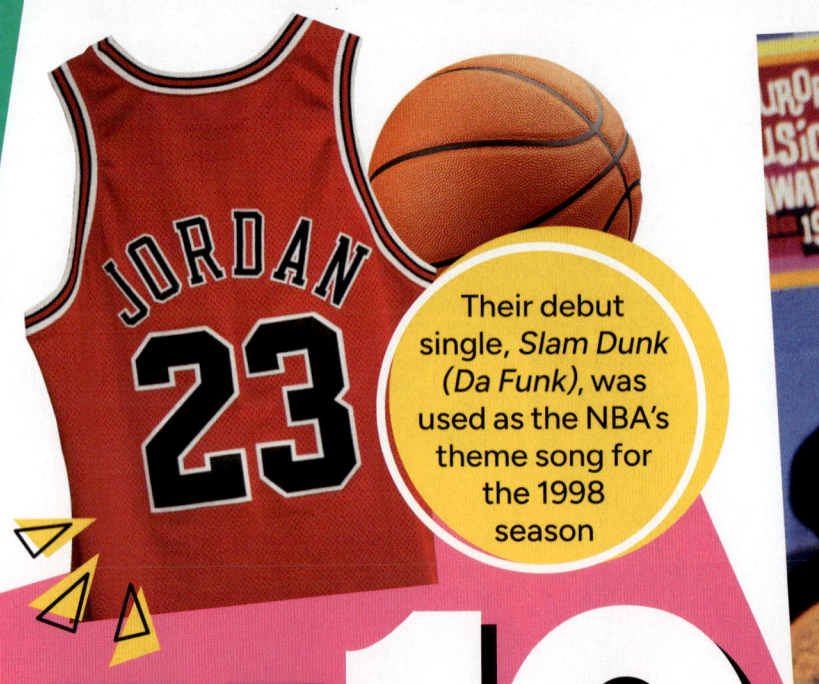

Their debut single, *Slam Dunk (Da Funk)*, was used as the NBA's theme song for the 1998 season

FIVE TOP 10

- Slam Dunk (Da Funk) (1997)
- When the Lights Go Out (1998)
- Got the Feelin' (1998)
- Everybody Get Up (1998)
- Until the Time Is Through (1998)
- If Ya Gettin' Down (1999)
- Keep On Movin' (1999)
- Don't Wanna Let You Go (1999)
- We Will Rock You (1999)
- Invincible (1999)

ICONIC

1997
FORMATION AND EARLY SUCCESS
Five was formed in 1997 after auditions held by Heart Management, the same team behind the Spice Girls.

1998
BREAKTHROUGH HIT
Their second single, *When the Lights Go Out*, became an international hit in 1998, peaking at number 10 on the Billboard Hot 100 in the United States. This song marked the first step to global stardom.

1998
DEBUT ALBUM SUCCESS
Their debut album, released in 1998, sold over 4 million copies worldwide. It included hits like *Got the Feelin'*, *Everybody Get Up* and *It's the Things You Do*.

With killer tracks and a cheeky grin, Five stormed the pop charts

At the MTV Europe Music Awards in 1998

SMASH HIT SUCCESS

Brit Award winners in 2000

SMASH HITS POLL WINNERS PARTY AWARDS
Five won the Best New Act Award in 1998 shortly after their debut.

MTV EUROPE MUSIC AWARDS
Showcasing their popularity across Europe, they won the Best UK & Ireland Act in 1999.

SILVER CLEF AWARD
Five received the Silver Clef Award in 1999 for their outstanding contribution to British music.

MORE SMASH HITS POLL WINNERS PARTY AWARDS
They were also recognised as the Best Band by Smash Hits readers in 1999 and they also received an award for Best Album for *Five*.

BRIT AWARD FOR BEST POP ACT
Five won this prestigious award at the Brit Awards in 2000. This was a major milestone for the band.

MOMENTS

1999
CHART-TOPPING SINGLES
In 1999, Five released *Keep On Movin'*, which became their biggest selling single and reached number one on the UK Singles Chart.

1999
ICONIC COLLABORATION
Fans went wild for their cover of Queen's *We Will Rock You*.

1999
SECOND ALBUM SUCCESS
Their second album, Invincible, released in 1999, sold over 1 million copies worldwide. It included hits like *Don't Wanna Let You Go* and *Invincible*.

J was marketed as the "bad boy" – but hated the persona!

The band were dynamic performers

PURE BLISS

What was it like to work for *Bliss* magazine? We asked esteemed editor Lisa Smosarski about the the early days of her career…

Lisa Smosarski

Hands up if you remember *Bliss* magazine? And keep your hand up if you would've sold your granny to work there in the 90s? Well, that's exactly where Lisa Smosarski, currently *Stylist's* editorial director, cut her teeth as a junior writer in 1998. Through hard work and talent of course – no relatives were sold – however Lisa does confirm that the world of *Bliss* was everything it was cracked up to be and more…

"What was my favourite part of my job?" Lisa ponders.

"God, I was just so delighted. I really was having a lovely time. I accidentally fell in, as you do in your first jobs, into the celebrity side…

"I felt like all my Christmases had come at once and I suddenly found myself in this world where I was invited to these showcases."

Showcases? Picture the scene. The era of boybands, and you're invited to see the latest up-and-coming talent perform their new music in front of a very select few people in some of the poshest venues. It was a world most of us could only dream of.

Lisa recalls one of the very first she attended, fresh out of university. Westlife hit the scene around the same time as her arrival at *Bliss* and were not only Lisa's first big interview, but she their first interviewer. Imagine! With everyone on the precipice of such exciting careers ahead, it was a magical time.

"Central London location, swishy venue. Going in, there were trays of black velvets, which are Champagne and Guinness, as a nod to Ireland," Lisa remembers.

"I just was so grateful for that opportunity, and so prepared to just say yes to everything and drink up every moment. Because you never know when that's going end, right?"

Of course, as with any perks, there came a staggering amount of hard work with lots of long hours and writing. And as well as that, a huge sense of responsibility to the readers, who weren't much younger than the writers themselves. Teen mags served as a link between fans and their idols, and that isn't something Lisa underestimates.

"There's a huge amount of evidence that a parasocial relationship can be as good for you as your own circle of friends.

"When you're going through your teen years where it's incredibly tumultuous, and you might be lonely, you might be experiencing friendship issues. You can actually lose yourself in these relationships, and they can give you as much as a friendship can.

"I think that's something I only came to understand later, but at the time, I was first hand witnessing these relationships. The readers would feel that they knew the celebrities. They cared about them. They would defend them vehemently if anyone

> **"The readers would feel that they knew the celebrities. They cared about them. They would defend them vehemently if anyone would say anything unkind about them!**

would say anything unkind about them!

"That's sometimes overlooked as sort of this kind of freaky fandom and girls being hysterical, or young adults being hysterical. But actually, I think that was a really important part of experimenting with our emotions, and actually feeling a connection and identity at a time when we're still figuring out our own identities.

"So I think for me and my role at *Bliss*, I was the facilitator between that relationship. How can I give them a little bit more of this friendship, or the relationship that they're building and the emotions that they're experimenting with."

Another thing Lisa remembers is the sheer volume of boyband talent rising through the ranks in this pocket of time. Of course, with different labels and PR, each band had different budgets and different reach. But as many other industry insiders can attest to, it really was the music that led to the biggest of successes.

"I think a good song and great choreography still were really critical. I don't think it was good enough to just be a set of young men who could sing and dance.

"I would have Louis Walsh calling me trying to place his acts and arranging something called playbacks. They were amazing.

"NSYNC were coming over to UK, I think it was for *I Want it that Way*.

"They wanted us desperately to cover it, but they couldn't release the single because they were scared of piracy! So I had to go and sit in the office with just three people while they played this song, really loud, trying to work out what to do with my face!

"Luckily, it was good. They played it three or four times on repeat, because they wanted to get to us early. Because I think if you could, if

Lisa's first big interview for *Bliss* – the wonderful Westlife!

there was a groundswell of support from fandoms, that fever passes on, doesn't it?"

It certainly does, and that fandom support often established boybands for years to come, with fans loyally pledging their allegiances to the likes of Take That or East 17.

And of course, it was teen magazines like *Bliss* who really fostered that support, ensuring readers knew everything there possibly was to know, and which hit was next!

With the boyband scene fit to bursting with talent, there was never a dull moment to be had in the magazine offices.

Between fielding record company calls and dealing with ginormous volumes of reader mail by the sack load, there was even occasional onsite entertainment!

"The bands would come and perform for you in the office" Lisa recalls.

"You'd have this stream of aspiring pop stars, all their dreams being made. You could see the light in their eyes, see they're really excited. This was their big break, coming through performing to offices of young women.

"Incredibly unusual experience, where you'd find pop stars singing and dancing *this* away from your face, and you're responding, yes, well done!

"That was my baptism into the working world. It was a completely unusual setup. It definitely speaks of a certain moment in time. I think that kind of big pop culture as well."

The life of a writer on a title such as *Bliss* magazine appears to have been a varied and exciting one full of possibility.

With young fans, young talent and young journalists, there truly was a sense of camaraderie.

"Everyone wanted to be there" says Lisa.

"In that 90s period, lots of these bands were launching, it was still super exciting.

"And I think some of the fatigue hadn't kicked in.

"There was just this huge sense of optimism."

So what do you think? Was a job at *Bliss* worth selling your granny for? We couldn't possibly say…

> **"In that 90s period, lots of these bands were launching, it was still super exciting. And I think some of the fatigue hadn't kicked in – there was just this huge sense of optimism"**

ULTIMATE WESTLIFE

Westlife closed out the 90s with a bang – sweet vocals, swoon-worthy smiles, and a string of unforgettable number ones

NAME GAME

Did you know that after the band dropped the name IOYOU, they were called Westside. They had to change their name again because another band had already nabbed it!

From Sligo to stardom, Westlife soared into hearts worldwide

From left, Brian, Mark, Nicky, Kian and Shane

The late 90s were no stranger to the boyband mania of the decade. In 1998, Sligo and Dublin in Ireland were proud to be home to Kian Egan, Markus Feehily, Nicky Byrne, Shane Filan and Brian McFadden – the five boys of course making up the globally recognised Westlife!

The band were famously managed by Louis Walsh and Ronan Keating and who better to advise the lads?

In 1999 they released their first single as Westlife, but their time together really started in 1997, originally named IOYOU. That 1999 single, Swear It Again, went straight to the top of the charts after the boys had built a loyal fanbase supporting the likes of Backstreet Boys and Boyzone on tour.

Following the single's success, Westlife released their self-titled album. In a fitting end to a decade blessed by boybands, I Have a Dream/Seasons in the Sun was the UK Christmas No.1, cementing their place in pop history.

This success in the latter part of the decade laid the foundations to their chart domination in the new millennium, with their next album, Coast to Coast, garnering triple Platinum status. Not bad for five lads from the west of Ireland!

In total, Westlife had 14 UK number one singles and sold 55 million records worldwide, which made their reunion in 2018 no surprise, with fans buying tickets to see the group once again in droves.

And this year, the band have confirmed new music and more live shows are on the horizon to mark the 25th anniversary of their first world tour. The light shines on! ▶▶

The band released their own Cadbury's chocolate bar in 2001!

Brian married then-Atomic Kitten singer Kerry Katona in January of 2002

WESTLIFE TOP 10

- I Have a Dream (1999)
- Flying Without Wings (1999)
- Swear It Again (1999)
- My Love (2000)
- When You're Looking Like That (2001)
- Uptown Girl (2001)
- Queen of My Heart (2001)
- World of Our Own (2002)
- You Raise Me Up (2005)
- What About Now (2009)

Performing at the Royal Variety in 1999

ICONIC

1998
FORMATION AND DEBUT
The band formed in Sligo. Their debut single *Swear It Again* topped UK charts.

1999
BREAKTHROUGH
The band scored hit after hit, achieving multiple UK No.1 singles.

2004
BRIAN DEPARTS
Brian left the band to focus on family and solo work. Westlife continued as a four-piece.

2008
CONTINUED FAME
Celebrated a decade together with a successful greatest hits tour.

2012
INITIAL SPLIT
After 14 years, Westlife announced their split following a farewell tour.

The fab five – always there to raise us up!

MOMENTS

2018
REUNION
Westlife reunited with new music and a tour. Their comeback single *Hello My Love* marked a fresh chapter.

Before his music career, Nicky played professional football…

…and hasn't lost his talent – he scored in Soccer Aid 2014!

SMASH HIT SUCCESS

Winning a Brit Award in 2001

BRIT AWARDS
With six nominations, Westlife took home Best Pop Act in 2001 and 2002.

METEOR IRELAND MUSIC AWARDS
A staggering 14 awards won between 2001 and 2008.

WORLD MUSIC AWARDS
The boys took the trophy for Best Irish Act in 2004.

MTV EUROPE MUSIC AWARD
Westlife won Best UK & Ireland Act in 2000.

RECORD OF THE YEAR
Another four wins for the band, for songs like *Flying Without Wings* and *You Raise Me Up*.

Wowing fans at the Record of the Year awards in 1999

BEHIND THE SCENES OF POP

From *Jackie* magazine to Take That tours, Ian McLeish's boyband-filled career was every teen's dream – and then some

Ian working hard in the office in the 90s

Meet Ian McLeish, the man who after reading this feature, you are likely to be insanely jealous of…

An expert in everything pop and a massively experienced journalist and editor, Ian started his career straight out of school at just 17 years old at DC Thomson-owned *Jackie* magazine in the late 80s, before working as pop editor on *Blue Jeans* magazine. After a stint back on *Jackie* as pop editor, Ian made the move down to London in the early 90s, and found himself in the centre of the boyband phenomenon of the decade.

"I moved down to London in 1994 to work on a magazine called *TV Hits*," explains Ian.

"It wasn't like the sort of height of the boybands, but when I came down to London, it absolutely exploded. I think the main thing to say is that everyone who worked on teen mags, more or less, were young, some in quite senior positions.

"I became editor of *TV Hits* when I was 23 or 24. You've got a lot of responsibility, but you're also in the mood to have fun, and everything is just a wild party, you know?

"I think what was really important was that a lot of the bands that we were interviewing were around the same age as us, so they kind of felt like they were your peers."

It was this almost 'colleague/friend' type environment that really fostered the relationship between boybands and teen magazines, with everyone chasing success, and having a great time in the process.

It also meant readers like us got the most incredible insight into our favourite stars from people who understood what we really wanted to know.

It was also during this time, both teen mags and the boybands featured began to understand the importance they both held to one another's success.

And Ian recalls that like the editorial staff, the boybands of the time weren't afraid of hard graft to build their fan bases.

"I remember there was a competition where we took some *Jackie* readers to Alton Towers or something like that, to meet Take That…" Ian remembers.

"Take That had this old Transit van that they piled into the back of and drove to the competition winner's house and picked them up!

"And you just think, those women now will have the most unbelievable stories that half their mates nowadays will just not believe happened.

"These people, Robbie Williams, Gary Barlow and so on, they became huge stars. But they turned up at their house and chapped the door and whisked them off.

"I think that the thing about Take That in particular, was that – and I don't mean this in a cynical way – they really played the game well. They recognised they were grafters. They really recognised that they needed to get all of the teen mags on side, and go on a bit of a charm offensive."

It was this fan knowledge, work ethic, alongside their later smash hits, that propelled bands like Take That into the history books forever.

Ian explains, "They really put the hours in, doing all the magazine road shows, charming all the staff, doing personal appearances and nightclubs up and down Britain.

"And it paid off because eventually they built up the fan base that when they had that song that was big enough to edge into the

With Gary Barlow!

80

Ian hung out with some of the biggest boybands of the time – including Boyzone!

charts, it just kind of went from there.

"I think that was a real example of the combination of hard work, having the right sort of characters in the band, but also the right song.

"The most important thing for me, what makes the really successful boybands, believe it or not, it's the songs. That's my takeaway anyway.

"You can build the best combination of who you think is the cheeky one and the cute one, but if the songs aren't there, they're not going to have any longevity.

Going on to work as editor of *Top of the Pops* magazine, Ian had a front row seat to the crazy world that boybands existed in. And with that came some pretty special experiences.

"What Take That used to do, which I think was genius, was the before any of their big arena tours, they would have a dress rehearsal just for the teen mags" Ian explains.

"So they would play like in

> "Take That had this old Transit van that they piled into the back of and drove to the competition winner's house and picked them up!

like 10,000 seater arena with literally 50 of us. They'd have a like sort of viewing platform thing, and they just had unlimited booze laid out on these tables, and you were there.

"The good thing about working in teen mags was that despite the fact that it was an extremely competitive market, by and large, we were all mates. It just felt like such a privilege, where they would go through the entire show, just for us."

Ian also had a front row seat to our favourite TV show.

"*Top of the Pops* was a really incredible experience" Ian goes on. "You would go down to Elstree for the filming of the show every week, and that was where we would get a lot of photo shoots too."

Not only did Ian and his colleagues have exclusive access, they also had the opportunity to travel too.

Ian recalls travelling as far as Hong Kong with Boyzone with an expectation that the band would feature prominently in his upcoming publications.

Of course, it goes without saying that with that hard work, came hard times too. At the end of the day, the boyband members were just young lads, away from their families with little to no time off.

"I was brutal" Ian agrees. "It was absolutely brutal. And obviously the biggest casualty of that was Robbie Williams. I remember I was in the room the first time he was in the same room as Take That after he'd split.

"I was in the audience, and he turned up, and it was a big shock that Robbie Williams was there, because he'd been avoiding that sort of confrontation."

Following Robbie's recent Netflix documentary and subsequent film, his struggles around that time have been well documented, and ring true for the experiences of many other boyband members.

However for the most part, Ian recalls a time of freedom, fun and a world full of opportunity for both those working in pop teen mags and boybands too.

So, there you have it, your suspicions confirmed. Working in the world of pop and teen mags in the 90s was truly all it was cracked up to be. Count us as jealous – and on the hunt for a time machine...

ULTIMATE BACKSTREET BOYS

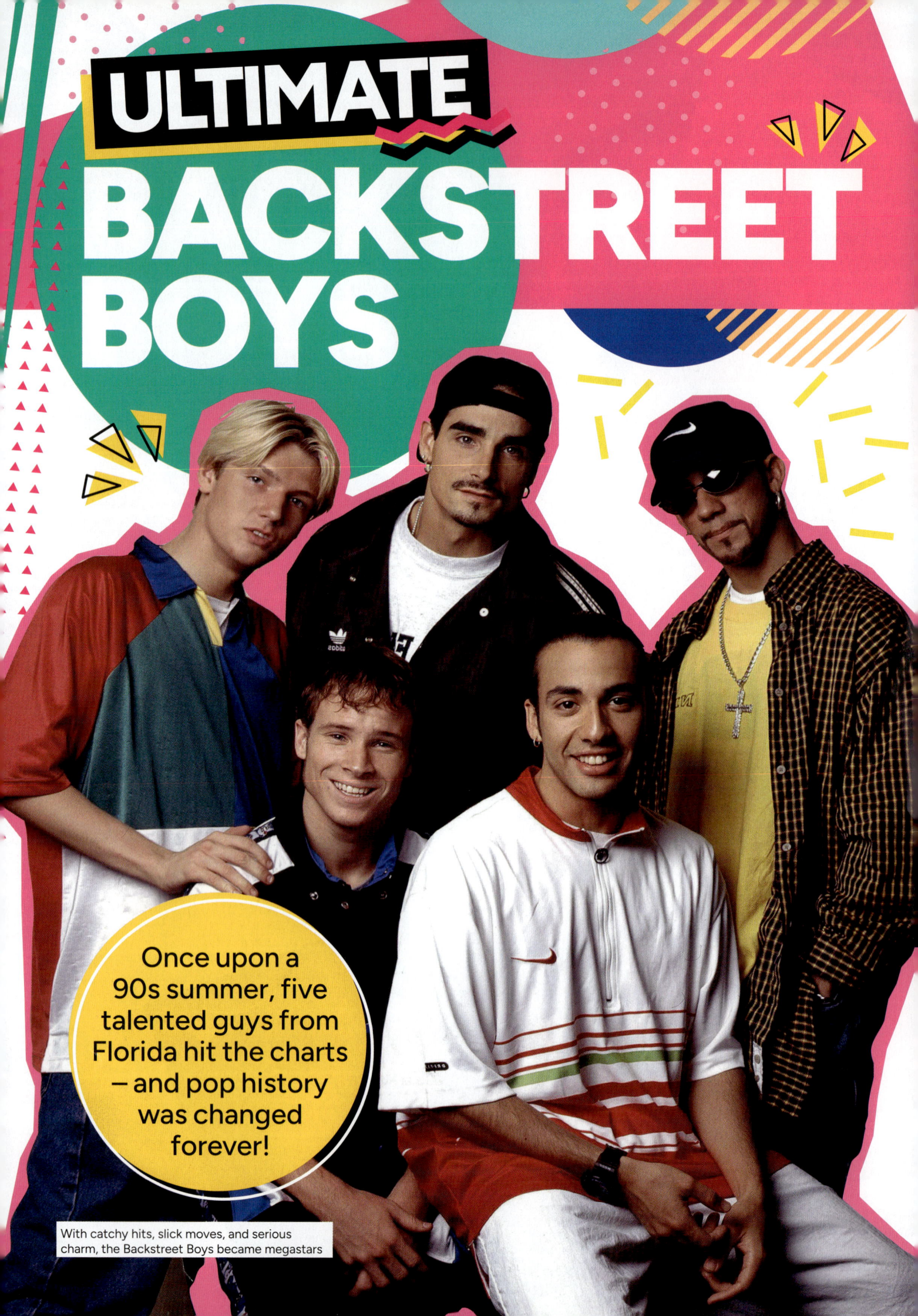

Once upon a 90s summer, five talented guys from Florida hit the charts – and pop history was changed forever!

With catchy hits, slick moves, and serious charm, the Backstreet Boys became megastars

In their prime, the Backstreet Boys didn't just make music – they made memories

DID YOU KNOW?

Ryan Gosling was almost a Backstreet Boy! AJ McLean invited him to join during a basketball game, but Gosling turned down the opportunity.

Ryan as a Backstreet Boy? We can see it!

It's no surprise that the Backstreet Boys skyrocketed to fame in the 90s. With their irresistible pop tunes, slick dance moves and dreamy looks, they were always destined for a place in the boyband Hall of Fame. Formed in 1993 in sunny Orlando, Florida, this fab five – AJ McLean, Howie Dorough, Nick Carter, Kevin Richardson, and Brian Littrell – were discovered by music mogul Lou Pearlman, who knew they were on course for global stardom.

In 1996 they burst on to the music scene with the release of their self-titled debut album which shot straight up the UK charts to the top 10. Their second album, *Backstreet's Back*, was released just a year later and gave us dancefloor hits like *Everybody (Backstreet's Back)* and *As Long As You Love Me*. By the mid-late 90s they were the ultimate crush for teens everywhere. Did you go head-over-heels for total hottie Kevin? Or were you more drawn to Brian and Howie's sweet and sensitive souls and their sobfest-inducing lyrics? Like so many of us, perhaps you just couldn't get enough of AJ's tats and bad boy vibe or Nick Carter – invariably the one who injected an extra shot of energy into every performance.

By the late 90s, the Backstreet Boys were household names. Their third album *Millennium*, released in 1999, was a mega-hit, featuring BSB classic *I Want It That Way*. While the band's success peaked in the 90s, the five have enjoyed continued success over the course of the last 30 years through various reunions and tours. Earlier this year the five drew a massive crowd at the Stagecoach Festival in the US, proving they can still bust those moves over three decades on. Backstreet's Back…or did it never really go away? ▶▶

Backstreet's back! The band are still wowing crowds in 2025

Kevin Richardson and Brian Littrell are actually cousins!

BACKSTREET BOYS TOP 10

- We've Got It Goin' On (1995)
- I'll Never Break Your Heart (1995)
- Quit Playing Games (With My Heart) (1996)
- Anywhere for You (1996)
- As Long As You Love Me (1997)
- All I Have to Give (1997)
- Everybody (Backstreet's Back) (1997)
- Larger Than Life (1999)
- I Want It That Way (1999)
- Show Me The Meaning of Being Lonely (1999)

The band filming the *Larger Than Life* music video in 1999

ICONIC

1996
DEBUT ALBUM SUCCESS IN THE UK
The Backstreet Boys' self-titled debut album was released in 1996 and became a massive hit in the UK, featuring tracks like *We've Got It Goin' On* and *Quit Playing Games (With My Heart)*.

1997
WINNING THE MTV EUROPE MUSIC AWARD FOR BEST GROUP
The Backstreet Boys won the MTV Europe Music Award for Best Group, elevating them to superstar status.

LATE 90s
PERFORMING AT THE SMASH HITS POLL WINNERS PARTIES
They performed at the iconic Smash Hits Poll Winners Party in the late 90s, a major event for UK pop music fans.

Big winners at the 1997 MTV Awards

SMASH HIT SUCCESS

They ruled the charts, dominated awards shows and stole our hearts

SMASH HITS AWARDS
In 1995 the group won the Best New Tour Act.

MTV EUROPE MUSIC AWARDS
In 1996 they won MTV Select for *Get Down (You're The One For Me)*.

BILLBOARD MUSIC AWARDS
The fabulous five won Group Album of the Year for *Backstreet Boys* in 1998.

MTV VIDEO MUSIC AWARDS
The group won a coveted MTV award for Best Group Video for *Everybody (Backstreet's Back)*.

SMASH HITS POLL WINNERS AWARDS
If Smash Hits deemed you to be cool then you were – sorted! The group were delighted to win Best Non-British Act in 1998.

BILLBOARD MUSIC AWARDS
The BSBs swept the Billboard awards in 1999 winning Album of the Year for *Millennium*, Album Artist Duo/Group of the Year, Album Artist of the Year and Artist of the Year.

MOMENTS

1997
EVERYBODY (BACKSTREET'S BACK) MUSIC VIDEO
The UK version of the *Everybody (Backstreet's Back)* music video became an instant classic with its Halloween-themed party iconic dance routines.

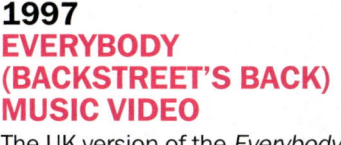

Nick Carter appeared as an extra in the 1990 film *Edward Scissorhands*

1999
MILLENNIUM ALBUM RELEASE
The release of their third album, *Millennium*, in 1999 was a pivotal moment. The album featured hits like *I Want It That Way* and *Larger Than Life* and it debuted at number two on the UK Album Chart.

Catchy hooks and co-ordinated outfits

DANCING QUEEN

Acclaimed hip-hop choreographer Fatima Robinson turned Backstreet Boys into the boyband that could really groove

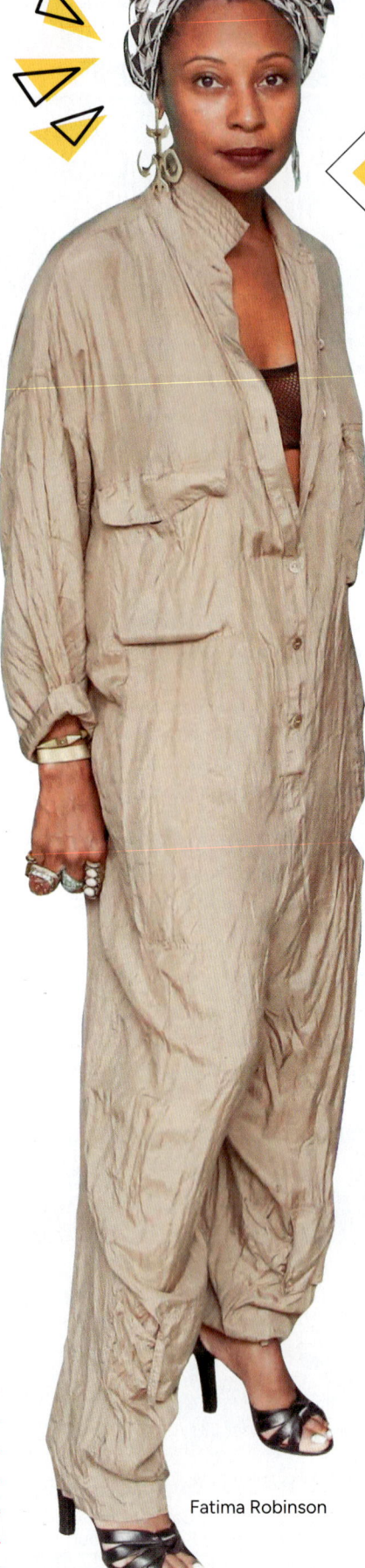

Fatima Robinson

Of all the successful boy bands from the 90s and noughties, one group totally stood out for their iconic dance moves and jaw-droppingly awesome videos. Who else but Backstreet Boys – AJ McLean, Howie Dorough, Nick Carter and cousins Kevin Richardson and Brian Littrell?

Their smooth, R&B influenced, story-based choreography set them apart and changed pop videos for ever. And this was entirely down to choreographer, Fatima Robinson.

A self-taught dance director and hip-hop goddess, in 1991 at the tender age of 21, she had choreographed Michael Jackson's epic Egyptian themed video *Do You Remember?*. She was in hot demand, dance directing for the likes of Mary J Blige, Bobby Brown and Aaliyah. Then, in 1995, she unexpectedly received a video tape in the post.

"It was from this random group of five white boys from Florida dancing and asking if I could choreograph them for a track called *Everybody (Backstreet's Back)*," she recalls.

"There was something so special about them. And I was like, they're kind of cool. They were really, really young and I just saw potential in them. I was getting off a Mary J. Blige tour, so I went to Orlando, and as we spent hours going over everything, I fell in love with each one of their personalities, their singing, and what they stood for."

Initially, inducting the boys into a hip-hop way of moving took a lot of work.

"They had never done my style before so it was kind of hard in the beginning for all of them. I'd go in and teach them something and then something would just not look right on them dancing. The quickest learner was definitely AJ – he was my little assistant.

"AJ and Howie were probably the most technically skilled dancers, Kevin and Brian brought stage presence and precision, and Nick provided the high-energy charisma. We just had a lot of fun.

"I always wanted to highlight their individual personalities because when you deal with groups like that, every girl or fan has their own particular favourite and you want to give each member equal shine. So, it was always, kinda, how do we highlight each personality and then bring them together as a group? As a dynamic whole?"

The band and Antonio Fargas in the *Everybody* music video

Fatima took inspiration from Michael Jackson when she choreographed the moves for *Everybody (Backstreet's Back)*. The dancing instantly became iconic with the haunted house setting giving way to a tight, stylised routine that was equal parts creepy and cool. The *Everybody* dance break with its sharp arm movements and synchronised footwork has gone down in boyband and indeed dance history as a game-changer.

"The inspiration came from my love for Michael, particularly his *Thriller* video. It was like my version of *Thriller*," Fatima revealed." I would never have believed those little steps would become so popular. I would sometimes make them up in my hotel room before rehearsal! The boys themselves had ideas and also there were times when they were like, 'Nah, not for us' about some of the moves."

The *Everybody (Backstreet's Back)* video is widely regarded as one of the most iconic boyband videos ever made. It solidified the

The iconic video was choreographed by Fatima

AJ McLean looking spooktacular!

A creepy Kevin Richardson during the shoot

Backstreet Boys' identity not just as singers but as all-around performers. It also marked a turning point where the visual storytelling in pop music – especially for male groups – got permission to be bigger, weirder and more ambitious. Fatima went on to choreograph the *As Long as You Love Me* video for the band, introducing a memorable chair routine that became another firm fan favourite.

However, her influence extended beyond Backstreet Boys' videos. She served as the choreographer on their Into the Millennium Tour in 1999 which featured elaborate staging and dance routines that captivated audiences worldwide.

BACKSTREET BOYS ARE BACK!

Although the band never officially split after the Millennium Tour, they went on something of a hiatus with the members pursuing separate projects. However currently they are back together and performing at their Into the Millennium residency at the Sphere entertainment venue in Las Vegas. This residency celebrates the 25th anniversary of their 1999 album *Millennium*. In conjunction with the residency, the Backstreet Boy released *Millennium 2.0* on July 11. This special edition commemorates the original album's 25th anniversary and includes remastered tracks, unreleased demos, live recordings, and a new single titled *Hey*.

Still going strong!

"Touring with them was amazing," she recalls. "And it kind of allowed me to travel a lot in Europe and really get to see the world, without having a lot to do. The band would be so busy during the day that we'd have only couple hour rehearsals here and there. And we really had a great time travelling all over the place."

Fatima who, post Backstreet Boys involvement, has gone on to work with – amongst others – Black Eyed Peas, Meghan Trainer and Beyonce, and also choreographed routines for the movies *Dream Girls* and the musical version of *The Color Purple*, says one of her proudest professional moments was watching the Backstreet Boys perform a medley of *Everybody (Backstreet's Back)* and *As Long As You Love Me* with 20 dancers at the 1997 MTV Europe Music Awards in the Netherlands.

"We were just the hit of the show," she says. "That was a really touching moment for me because I had been with them since day one. I'm really happy that I took the job and that I became part of their lives. I mean, I saw them grow up."

ULTIMATE NSYNC

They came from Disney and dance studios, but NSYNC became the kings of teen pop with charm and catchy tunes

NSYNC TOP 10

- Tearin' up My Heart (1997)
- I Want You Back (1998)
- Thinking of You (I Drive Myself Crazy) (1999)
- (God Must Have Spent) A Little More Time on You (1999)
- Bye Bye Bye (2000)
- It's Gonna Be Me (2000)
- This I Promise You (2000)
- Pop (2001)
- Gone (2001)
- Girlfriend (2002)

Justin, JC, Joey, Lance and Chris – five names, one unforgettable era

SMASH HIT SUCCESS

WALK OF FAME
In 2018, NSYNC were awarded a star on the Hollywood Walk of Fame. The star was dedicated in the category of Recording at 7080 Hollywood Boulevard.

ICONIC MOMENTS

1998
THE DISNEY CHANNEL CONCERT SPECIAL
NSYNC took part in a Disney Channel concert in 1998 that would see a huge boost to their popularity across America.

1998
OPENING FOR JANET JACKSON
In October 1998 the band joined Janet Jackson's Velvet Rope World Tour, opening for her at the Baltimore Arena in Maryland.

2001
SUPERBOWL
The band played the 2001 Superbowl, alongside the likes of Britney Spears and Aerosmith.

2002
OLYMPICS
NSYNC performed at the 2002 Winter Olympics in Utah's Salt Lake City in the US, delighting fans across the world.

2013
MTV MUSIC AWARDS
They reunited for a long-awaited performance at the 2013 MTV Music Awards.

2024
SURPRISE REUNION
In 2024, the group performed together for the first time in over 10 years when Justin Timberlake brought his former bandmates out on stage during a concert in Los Angeles.

MTV Award winners in 2000!

MTV VIDEO MUSIC AWARDS
The band won multiple MTV Video Awards in 2000 and 2001, with the videos for *Girlfriend, Gone, Pop, Bye Bye Bye* and *Tearin' up My Heart* winning in the categories of Best Pop Video, Best Choreography, Viewer's Choice Awards, Best Dance Video and Best Group Video.

BILLBOARD MUSIC AWARD
In 2000 the boys won a Billboard Music Award for the Top Billboard 200 Album with their album *No Strings Attached*. The album debuted at number one on the Billboard 200 and sold 2.4 million copies in its first week, setting a record for the largest sales week for an album.

PEOPLE'S CHOICE AWARD FOR FAVOURITE GROUP
In both 2001 and 2002, NSYNC won the People's Choice Award for Favourite Group.

AMERICAN MUSIC AWARD FOR FAVOURITE DUO OR GROUP POP/ROCK
They were firm fan favourites, and in 2002 won the American Music Award for Favourite Duo or Group Pop/Rock.

With their raw musical talent, flawless choreography and undeniable good looks, NSYNC were one of the most iconic bands of the 90s. The band formed in 1995, the name NSYNC an acronym using the last letter of each member's first name. The band brought together stars from the much-loved children's TV show *The Mickey Mouse Club* Justin Timberlake and JC Chasez, who were joined by Joey Fatone, then a performer at Orlando's Universal Studios, high school chorister Lance Bass and Chris Kirkpatrick of music group the Hollywood Hi-Tones.

While the band are American, they initially found fame in Europe. They were first signed by RCA/BMG Germany and their debut album, *NSYNC*, was released in Germany in 1997. A successful tour of Europe followed.

When NSYNC's debut album was released in the US in 1998, it was number two within six months. The next couple of years would be the biggest for the band, seeing the release of award-winning albums *No Strings Attached* and *Celebrity*, accompanied by sell-out tours.

They had won over the US and were breaking the hearts of teenage girls across the States.

Fans were devastated when the band took a hiatus in 2002. Some say the launch of Justin Timberlake's solo career was the reason for the band's effective break-up.

In 2007 the band's break-up was officially confirmed, but they have reunited on several occasions for one-off gigs, including at the 2013 MTV Video Music Awards and, somewhat bizarrely, in 2023 for a cameo in kids film *Trolls Band Together*.

One of the world's most popular boybands, these 90s heartthrobs continue to hold a place in many of our hearts.

ULTIMATE HANSON

MMMBop made them stars, but these boyband brothers were so much more!

The band grew up together, sang together and soared to stardom

Taylor, Zac and Isaac in 2000

Alongside their music, the Hanson brothers have ventured into other avenues, including owning their own brewery! The Hanson Brothers Beer Co's first release was a citrusy IPA called MMMHops. Three cheers to that!

Unlike many of the boybands of the era, Hanson didn't come together through management or even through friendship – these bandmates were together since birth!

Brothers Isaac, Taylor and Zac Hanson first sang a cappella in the early 90s, recording classic covers such as *Johnny B. Good* and *Rockin' Robin*. Their first official performance was in 1992, when the boys were just 11, 9 and 6 respectively.

The band is headed up by middle brother and lead singer Taylor, with elder brother Isaac on guitar and backing vocals, and Zac playing percussion. They recorded their first two albums in Tulsa, their hometown, but it wasn't until 1997 that the brothers got their breakthrough.

MMMBop was the track that launched a teenage Hanson to stardom, reaching number one in 14 countries with its catchy, singalong melody. One critic once likened the earworm it gave him to gum getting stuck on a shag carpet!

Following a bout of 'creative differences' with their label after their initial success, Hanson formed their own label 3GC Records in 2003. Their release of their third album *Underneath* a year later was the main topic of their documentary film *Strong Enough to Break*, which followed the struggles the band faced when releasing it. The record hit number 1 on Billboard's US Independent Albums Chart.

Still active today, Hanson have spoken about the pride of their origins, and the fact they 'came up' in the 90s, and are known for being down-to-earth despite their success.

DID YOU KNOW?

In 2016, MTV reporter Patrick Hosken counted approximately 93,000 cover versions of *MMMBop*! One notable cover came from noughties boyband Busted, who collaborated with Hanson on *MMMBop 2.0*.

Busted

ULTIMATE BOYZ II MEN

Boyz II Men are a soul/R&B group who were established back in 1985 and are still active today, although they reached their peak in the 90s. The band currently consists of singers Nathan Morris, Wanyá Morris and Shawn Stockman. In the 90s, they had a fourth member in Mike McCary, but he left in 2003 due to health issues. Boyz II Men have enjoyed huge chart-topping success and became only the third group after The Beatles and Elvis to replace themselves at the top of the Billboard Hot 100.

With velvet harmonies and timeless ballads, Boyz II Men defined 90s R&B – and they're still singing their hearts out today

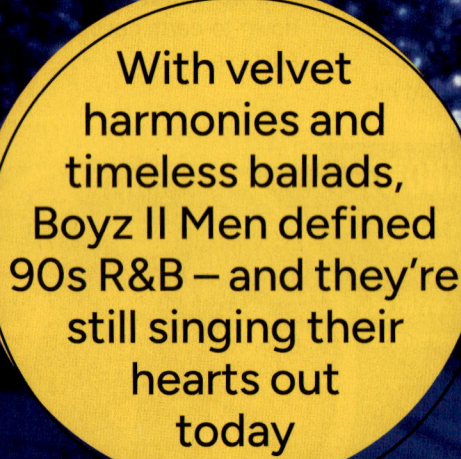

The band dazzled in their 90s heyday

From left, Shawn Stockman, Nathan Morris, Wanya Morris and Mike McCary in 1992

EARLY SUCCESS

The band's first few singles were an instant success. In 1991, they released *Motownphilly* and *It's So Hard to Say Goodbye to Yesterday* which both peaked in the top five on the Billboard Hot 100. Perhaps their most iconic single *I'll Make Love To You* was a staggering success when it came out in 1994 as the lead single from their second album *II*, which followed their debut *CooleyHighHarmony* in 1991.

Some other successful singles included *End of The Road*, which set a record at the time of 13 weeks spent at the top of the Hot 100 in 1992.

Track *One Sweet Day*, which was a collaboration with Mariah Carey, also spent a whopping 16 weeks at number one.

In 1999, Boyz II Men were resigned to UMG's Universal Records from Motown, who were bought over, and the group released *Nathan Michael Shawn Wanya* under the new label.

However, the band departed from Universal shortly afterwards in 2001.

By 2004, they had established MSM Music Group and began releasing records under the label, starting with *Throwback, Vol. 1*.

Just like its name suggests, the album was a collection of classic R&B covers and included hits such as The Dazz Band's *Let It Whip*, Michael Jackson's *Human Nature* and Bobby Caldwell's track, *What You Won't Do for Love*.

WHERE ARE THEY NOW?

Now, Boyz II Men are still regularly touring with one on the go currently across the USA, plus some stops in Asia.

Will we get new music from them anytime soon? Only time can tell…

BOYZ II MEN ALBUMS

To this date, Boyz II Men have released 12 studio albums with the latest out in 2017:

▶ **Cooleyhighharmony (1991)**
▶ **Christmas Interpretations (1993)**
▶ **II (1994)**
▶ **Evolution (1997)**
▶ **Nathan Michael Shawn Wanya (2000)**
▶ **Full Circle (2002)**
▶ **Throwback, Vol. 1 (2004)**
▶ **Winter/Reflections (2005)**
▶ **The Remedy (2006)**
▶ **Motown: A Journey Through Hitsville USA (2007)**
▶ **Love (2009)**
▶ **Covered: Winter (2010)**
▶ **Twenty (2011)**
▶ **Collide (2014)**
▶ **Under the Streetlight (2017)**

A NEW CHAPTER

SOLO SUCCESS

ROBBIE WILLIAMS, TAKE THAT

Robbie's career kicked off in Take That when the band formed in 1990, and he stayed until his dramatic departure in 1995. He sang vocals for the group during his time with them before releasing his debut solo album two years later, named *Life Thru a Lens*.

Williams' experience as part of Take That was far from simple, he confessed on the BBC documentary *Boybands Forever*.

As the youngest member of the group – alongside bandmates Gary Barlow, Mark Owen, Jason Orange, and Howard Donald – Williams admitted his strained relationship with their manager at the time, Nigel Martin-Smith.

"The early days of Take That were spent in rehearsals. I had no dance background and the routines were so intricate so I would have trouble picking up the steps which would make me look like I was being lazy," he said.

"This was brought up in not a favourable way. Let's just say Nigel wasn't very happy with my application."

However, upon going solo, Williams experienced overwhelming success with hit songs including *Angels, Rock DJ, Let Me Entertain You, Candy, Feel* and *She's The One*.

He has released 13 studio albums as a solo artist, with another named *BRITPOP* on its way this autumn.

Plus, in 2024, Williams starred in his own biopic entitled *Better Man*.

The star is now 51 and still working hard!

DID YOU KNOW?

- He has won the most Brit Awards out of any artists in history, with a record 13 as a solo artist and five with Take That!
- He appeared in an episode of *EastEnders* in 1995, just before he left Take That.
- Williams had his own clothing line which had a short run from 2011-13.
- Before becoming a singer, Williams worked as a salesman in his hometown of Stoke-on-Trent.
- He voiced the character of Dougal in *The Magic Roundabout Movie*.
- He's a 12-time Official Albums Chart-topper.

They shared the stage, now they walk alone — five boyband favourites who struck out solo

Timberlake's work as an actor includes roles in children's move franchise *Trolls*

JUSTIN TIMBERLAKE, NSYNC

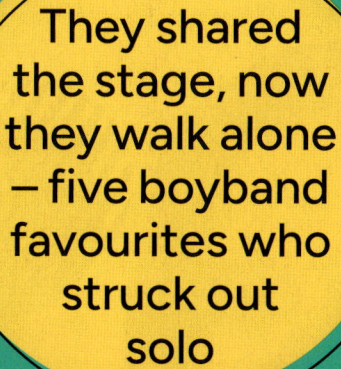

Justin Timberlake has enjoyed a fruitful career as a solo artist, as well as starring in various acting roles, since performing as part of NSYNC. From Memphis, Tennessee, Timberlake is now dubbed the Prince of Pop after his glittering career started in 1995.

During his days in NSYNC, Timberlake performed lead vocals alongside bandmates JC Chasez, Chris Kirkpatrick, Lance Bass and Joey Fatone. Together, the fivesome produced four studio albums and some global smash hit singles including *Bye Bye Bye* and *It's Gonna Be Me*.

Timberlake's solo debut came out back in 2002 during the band's hiatus. It was entitled *Justified* and caused a ripple effect in the pop industry, making him a superstar in his own right upon its release. He turned to R&B for the album and rewrote his image from teenage pop idol to a mature megastar.

Since then, Timberlake has made six studio albums with hits including *SexyBack*, *Can't Stop The Feeling* and *Cry Me a River*. ▶▶

DID YOU KNOW?

- Justin Timberlake has famously dated both Britney Spears and Cameron Diaz in the past.
- He was only 14 years old when NSYNC started.
- *Justified* won him his first Grammy — for Best Pop Vocal Album.
- Once, in 2002, he broke his foot during dance rehearsals!
- His father was a choir director at a Baptist church.

The old gang back together last year

MARK OWEN, TAKE THAT

Another beloved member of Take That is Mark Owen, and although he remains part of the band, he still managed to kickstart a solo career back in 1996. Between then and now, he has released five studio albums. Owen's debut album was *Green Man*, released just after the band first split up.

He had previously joined forces with the other members in 1989 and has managed to sell 45 million records with them.

But as part of his debut, Owen managed to land a top three hit *Child*.

Altogether, Owen has had three UK top ten hits. He's never had a number one album, but his most recent record did reach the top ten in 2022.

Owen's full list of studio albums are *Green Man* (1996), *In Your Own Time* (2003), *How the Mighty Fall* (2005), *The Art of Doing Nothing* (2013) and *Land of Dreams* (2022).

DID YOU KNOW?

- Owen grew up in Oldham, Lancashire, living in a council house with his family.
- He auditioned for Take That at just 17 years old.
- He had no professional musical training before joining – the only credibility he had was performing in school shows.
- Owen sang lead vocals on several Take That hits including *Shine*, *Up All Night* and *Babe*.
- Owen hasn't toured as a solo act since 2013.
- Owen won series two of *Celebrity Big Brother*, which aired in 2001.
- He has been married to his wife Emma Ferguson since 2009.

RONAN KEATING, BOYZONE

Ronan Keating is an Irish singer who rose to prominence from 1993 as part of Boyzone. Some key hits from the band, which he played in alongside members Mikey Graham, Keith Duffy, Shane Lynch and Stephen Gately, include *No Matter What, Every Day I Love You, All That I Need* and *Picture of You*. The band, managed by Louis Walsh, was originally envisioned as an "Irish Take That".

However, Keating's success didn't end with the band. Instead, he's produced 10 solo studio albums up until now, with the first one, *Ronan*, coming out in 2001. Afterwards he released *Destination* (2002), *Turn It On* (2003), *Bring You Home* (2006), *Songs For My Mother* (2009), *Winter Songs* (2009), *When Ronan Met Burt* (2011), *Fires* (2012), *Time of My Life* (2016), and *Songs From Home* (2021).

His hit song *When You Say Nothing at All* (also his debut solo single) famously featured in the 1999 romcom *Notting Hill*, which starred Hugh Grant opposite Julia Roberts. After the track peaked at number one in the UK charts, Keating's solo career was off to a flying start.

He also took stints managing other bands and writing music for them after the success of *Ronan*, which eventually went four-times platinum. His latter albums included A-list collaborations with the likes of Elton John, Lulu and the Bee Gees.

Keating has also appeared as an *X Factor* judge in Australia and as an actor in various small roles in film.

DID YOU KNOW?

Keating was only 16 when he joined Boyzone.

He was awarded the Ivor Novello Award for songwriting for *Picture of You* in 1996.

He performed at the 2006 FIFA World Cup opening party in front of millions worldwide.

In 2016, Keating replaced Ricky Martin as a judge on *The Voice Australia*.

He also joined BBC's *The One Show* as co-host in 2021.

Keating was the voice of the character Harris in *PAW Patrol: The Movie*.

Due to his extensive charity work, Keating was awarded an honorary degree by the Open University in 2022.

BRIAN MCFADDEN, WESTLIFE

Westlife's Brian McFadden, another Irish boyband superstar, went solo in 2004. He'd been part of Westlife between 1998 and 2004 but left to spend more time with his family and work on solo music.

Westlife consisted of McFadden, Nicky Byrne, Shane Filan and Kian Egan who formed together in Sligo. By 2012 they'd disbanded but, like Take That, they reunited in 2018. The group managed to achieve 11 number one albums in their peak and 16 number one singles, making them one of the most popular UK boybands of the 90s.

However, McFadden did more with his career after Westlife. His debut solo single, *Real to Me*, came out in 2004 followed the album, *Irish Son*, which peaked in the top ten of the official Irish Albums Chart.

He has released five studio albums with the most recent one coming out in 2019. After *Irish Son*, there was *Set in Stone* (2008), *Wall of Soundz* (2010), *The Irish Connection* (2013) and finally *Otis*.

Alongside his solo music, McFadden has taken up work as a TV presenter and judge on *Australia's Got Talent*, since he now lives over there. He also hosted the UK show *Who's Doing the Dishes?*.

Plus, he joined forces with Boyzone singer Keith Duffy to form BoyzLife! The pair have since toured together.

DID YOU KNOW?

His younger sister is a theatre star and gained traction for playing Sandy in *Grease* and Elle Woods in *Legally Blonde: The Musical* on the West End.

McFadden was married to Atomic Kitten singer Kerry Katona, tying the knot in 2002. They divorced in 2006 and share two daughters.

He is popular in Australia and is signed up with Universal Music Australia.

He changed his name from Brian to Bryan so it would be easier to sign autographs.

10 BEST BOYBAND HITS OF THE 90s

...in no particular order!

1. WHEN THE GOING GETS TOUGH BOYZONE (1999)

Comic Relief 1999 was the jumping off point for this charity cover of Billy Ocean's 1985 hit. The music video tipped its hat to the original, featuring UK celebrities lip syncing along, and became one of the most successful Comic Relief singles of all time!

2. TEARIN' UP MY HEART NSYNC (1998)

Lance Bass once said that *Tearin' Up My Heart* was a more energetic version of *I Want You Back*. The track built on the success of its successor, helping NSYNC to solidify their sound – and their place in the hearts of many!

3. SWEAR IT AGAIN WESTLIFE (1999)

It's a rare thing for a debut single to hit the number one spot, but *Swear It Again* was just that good. Surprisingly, the track is Westlife's fifth-best-selling-single, but the only one to have charted in the US, hitting number 20 at its peak.

4. WE WILL ROCK YOU FIVE (1999)

Five's cover of Queen's *We Will Rock You* mixed in some of their trademark rapping to roaring success. Brian May and Roger Taylor reprised their roles on guitar and drums on the single, in the music video and even on a Brits performance in 2000.

5. NO MATTER WHAT BOYZONE (1998)

Boyzone's version of Andrew Lloyd Webber and Jim Steinham's song swapped the religious leanings of the musical original to a teenage love song. Boyzone's reinterpretation paid off, as their *Whistle Down the Wind* cover became the band's fourth number one.

6. BACK FOR GOOD TAKE THAT (1995)

When *Back for Good* was released, rumours circulated that the Bee Gees' Barry Gibb penned the song in secret. The track was, in fact, the work of Gary Barlow, and he remarkably wrote it in just 15 minutes!

7. MMMBOP HANSEN (1997)

Joyous and jovial, *MMMBop* is, in fact, a bop! It may be difficult to imagine, but this track had a slower and darker sound that didn't resonate with record labels. Mercury eventually picked up the track and saw it transformed into the singalong song we know and love!

8. I HAVE A DREAM WESTLIFE (1999)

Westlife's fourth single – an ABBA cover – was the last chart-topper of the 90s, beating out Cliff Richard's *The Millenium Prayer*. The group rerecorded the track in 2001 to raise funds for UNICEF, featuring Indonesian child singer Sinna Sherina Munaf.

9. STEP BY STEP NEW KIDS ON THE BLOCK (1990)

New Kids on the Block's biggest international hit started life as a flop released by The Superiors in 1987. NKOTB's rerecording was a smash success, which marked a tonal shift as the band transitioned from their teenage sound to something more mature.

10. I WANT YOU BACK NSYNC (1996)

NSYNC's first single was first released in Germany in 1996, where it charted at number 10. The track wasn't released in the US until 1997, and the UK until 1999, but the quadruple gold track was critical in putting NYSNC on the international stage.

103

A master songwriter and performer

1992

Following the initial split of Take That in 1996, it wasn't long before Gary Barlow embarked on a solo career that showcased his incredible vocal and songwriting talents.

His debut solo album *Open Road* topped the UK album chart in 1997 and gave fans memorable hits such as *Forever Love* and *Love Won't Wait*.

However, as we moved into the late 90s and musical tastes shifted, Gary Barlow's solo momentum slowed.

After a quieter few years Take That reunited in 2005, which boosted Gary's profile again massively. Alongside the group's huge success, he also flourished individually – writing for artists like Elton John, Shirley Bassey, and former bandmate Robbie Williams, quickly becoming one of the most respected figures in British music.

His 2013 solo album *Since I Saw You Last* marked a triumphant return as a solo artist, featuring the hit single *Let Me Go*.

In recent years, Barlow has diversified, and as as well as his own solo stage performances, he's also got involved in a variety of other projects including *Calendar Girls: The Musical* and his wine brand, Gary Barlow Wines.

This year, he's celebrating his four-decade-spanning career with The Songbook Tour, a 41-date UK tour that revisits his greatest hits from both his solo work and Take That.

Now a beloved national treasure, Gary Barlow's solo success is defined not just by chart-topping hits, but by his enduring influence as a songwriter, performer and creative force in British music. ▶▶

Reuniting with Robbie!

At Windsor Castle with Andrew Lloyd Webber for the Queen's Diamond Jubilee

GARY TOP 10

- Forever Love (1996)
- Love Won't Wait (1997)
- So Help Me Girl (1997)
- Open Road (1997)
- Hang On in There Baby (with Rosie Gaines) (1998)
- Stronger (1999)
- For All That You Want (1999)
- Shame (with Robbie Williams) (2010)
- Sing (with The Commonwealth Band) (2012)
- Face to Face (with Elton John) (2014)
- Since I Saw You Last (2014)

ICONIC

1996
DAZZLING DEBUT
Forever Love, Gary's first solo single, rocketed straight to the number one spot in the UK charts.

1997
FANTASTIC FOLLOW-UP
Riding high on that solo success, Gary's second single *Love Won't Wait* also went to number one in the charts.

2010
OLD PALS ACT
Shame – fans loved this reconciliation duet with Robbie Williams and the song made it all the way to number two.

2012
SING SUCCESS
Co-written with Andrew Lloyd Webber for the Queen's Diamond Jubilee, *Sing* was performed with the Commonwealth Band and reached number one. Gary also performed at the Buckingham Palace celebration for the Diamond Jubilee.

A special duet with Elton in 2013

MOMENTS

2014
ELTON DUET
Gary teamed up with fellow musical icon Elton John to perform a duet of *Face to Face* – a song celebrating friendship and resilience.

2020
MORE COLLABS
Gary teamed up with Michael Bublé and Sebastián Yatra to create a Latin-pop collaboration when they sung *Elita* together.

2021
TOUR TIME
Gary embarked on his Music Played by Humans Tour – a special set if concerts following the orchestral album that debuted at number one.

With Michael Bublé

SMASH HIT SUCCESS

Receiving his OBE in 2013

IVOR NOVELLO AWARDS
In 1997, Gary bagged two Ivor Novello Awards – one for Best Contemporary Song for *Back for Good* (written for Take That, but awarded during his solo period) and also Songwriter of the Year where he was recognised for his songwriting excellence during the early phase of his solo career.

MUSIC INDUSTRY TRUSTS AWARD
In 2012 he was honoured for his outstanding contribution to British music and charity work. He also won a Classic Brit Award – Best Album for *Sing*, the Diamond Jubilee record co-written with Andrew Lloyd Webber.

OBE
In 2013 Gary was awarded an OBE in the Queen's Birthday Honours for services to the entertainment industry and charity.

UK ALBUMS CHART
In 2021 Gary's *Music Played by Humans* debuted at number one on the UK album chart, marking a major solo achievement.

At the Ivor Novellos in 1997

Five things you might not know about Five

1 Five were one of few British boy bands who broke America. Their 1998 single *When the Lights Go Out* peaked at number 10 on the Billboard Hot 100 and remained on the chart for six months, while their debut album, *Five*, reached number 27 on the Billboard 200 and went platinum.

TAKE FIVE

As 90s boyband Five reunite for a massive UK arena tour, we look back at their incredible success – and the tears and traumas that led to their split

2. Five things you might not know about Five

There was a sixth member of the band at one point, but he was cut before they were launched.

It's hard to believe that it's been 28 years since boyband Five first burst onto the music scene with ridiculously catchy, chart-topping hits such as *When The Lights Go Out*, *If Ya Gettin' Down* and *Keep On Moving*.

Signed by a then little known Simon Cowell to create "chaos", Five were the antithesis of the clean cut, boy-next-door style boybands of the time. All hoodies, hair gel and huge egos, Abs Love, Jason "J" Brown, Richie Neville, Scott Robinson and Sean Conlon were the edgier big brothers of Boyzone and Westlife – something that proved a recipe for huge success.

After hitting the charts with their debut single *Slam Dunk (Da Funk)*, which made a big splash in the Top 10, their faces were soon plastered over teenage bedrooms across the UK. Three smash hit albums later and over 10 million records sold worldwide, they decided to go their separate ways – much to the devastation of their fans.

The split came in 2001, four years after they formed, amid rumours of burnout, mental breakdown and backstage fights. It was something that they spoke openly about last year in *Boybands Forever*, a three-part BBC documentary about the golden age of manufactured bands in the 1990s and early 2000s.

In it, Richie reflected on the darker aspects of fame, including exploitation, lack of personal freedom, and the need for better mental health support for young artists. Specifically, he talked about how the band were overworked and overwhelmed, with only two days off in two years during the early part of their success, and how being in a boyband could feel like a "prison sentence".

He recounted an incident where, after contracting chickenpox while touring Australia and New Zealand, a label representative dismissed medical advice for rest, saying, "Doctors over-exaggerate, don't they?" People often don't get it… They think being in a famous band is a dream."

Five things you might not know about Five

3 Their first audition was a disaster. They were told to look "streetwise and cheeky". So they got drunk, trashed a hotel room, and yelled insults at the executives. Simon Cowell loved it and signed them.

▶▶ Other members have also spoken openly about the pressures.

"On stage we were the best ever. Off stage we were a train wreck," said Scott. "Life in Five was mental. It was years of very hard work. You see the inside of a hotel room, an airport, a radio studio. It's hard."

In the end, the boys gave up caring, with Ritchie and J getting arrested for a bar fight in Dublin which they hoped would anger their bosses. But Ritchie recalls, "The phone rings and it's Simon Cowell… But his exact words were, 'Well done, you can't buy publicity like that. This is amazing'."

After the band split, things didn't get much better; three of the boys – Abz, Sean and Richie – have spoken about experiencing severe mental health issues such as depression and anxiety, and battles with drugs and alcohol. Just over a decade later, they reformed as part of ITV2 reality series *The Big Reunion*, alongside fellow pop giants Atomic Kitten, B*Witched, 9-1-1, Liberty X, and The Honeyz.

With such bad memories from their years at the top, it seems surprising, then, that the boys (or should that be, men, as the band are all now in their 40s) should want to reunite. But that's exactly what they plan to do.

In October 2025, they will embark on a 25-date UK arena tour, visiting cities like London, Bournemouth, Nottingham, Liverpool and Glasgow – something that's been a long time in the planning, with more than 18 months of secret meet-ups to nail down their plans. But thankfully, they've all been getting along famously, with the old tensions firmly put behind them.

"The second we saw each other, it was magical," said Scott, now 45, at a press conference announcing the reunion in February. Abz, also 45, confirmed, "Within the first second of seeing each other, it was like none of it mattered anymore."

With the lads now more mature – not only in attitude but in years – can we expect the same high-energy routines on stage as in their heyday, though?

"We're not going as far as backflips," laughed J, 48, "but it is actually kind of embarrassing how much energy we're going to bring."

Abz jokingly added, "I might have an oxygen tank and sick bucket at the side of the stage, just in case."

In 2013 Five reformed as part of ITV2 reality series *The Big Reunion*, but without J – who watched on from home, shocked by accusations of 'bullying' which he has categorically denied

4 Five things you might not know about Five

The boys almost sabotaged their own success by rejecting tracks that went on to be hits for other artists – including *...Baby One More Time*, which of course made Britney Spears a superstar, and an early version of *Bye Bye Bye*, which later became a hit for NSYNC.

5 Five things you might not know about Five

The boys often came to blows with manager Simon. Scott has revealed that, on one occasion, he almost ended up in a fist fight with him. "I'd lost my mind," he says. "They had to call security and carry me out of the building kicking and screaming", while Simon has confirmed, "I was that close to punching him in the face."

WHERE ARE THEY NOW?

NATHAN MORRIS

Boyz II Men are a much-loved 90s group who are still gigging and recording music today. However, for founding member and vocalist Nathan Morris, this is something he now juggles with a more recently founded career in real estate. In 2018, Nathan launched the HGTV reality series *Hit Properties with Nathan Morris*, which saw the star transform dilapidated properties across the US into luxury accommodation. While this only lasted for one series, Morris continues to operate as a successful real estate investor and developer.

In recent years he has also spoken publicly about a newfound love of fitness, which saw him lose almost three stone at the age of 46. Alongside his now strict fitness regime, he is currently working with his fellow bandmates on developing a feature film biopic and a documentary about Boyz II Men, with a release date yet to be confirmed.

The soul stars with Nathan, second left

The band were honoured with a star on the Hollywood Walk Of Fame in 2012

From 90s heartthrobs to...? Just where are the famous faces we once knew so well?

Most of us will remember the famous faces from 90s boybands as we knew them back then: fresh-faced and at the height of their fame. But where are they now? Some have continued in their music careers, many have forged new careers for themselves, and others have disappeared from the public eye entirely.

LEE BRENNAN

After 911's split in 2000, frontman Lee Brennan carved a new career for himself. Finding a passion in acting, he has appeared in various stage shows, including a run playing the part of Willard in stage productions of *Footloose: The Musical*. He has also appeared in productions of *Sleeping Beauty, Beauty and the Beast, Peter Pan* and *Aladdin*.

However, his days with 911 weren't behind him. In 2013 the band re-formed alongside the likes of Atomic Kitten, B*Witched and Blue for the ITV documentary *The Big Reunion*. Off the back of this, the band continued to perform gigs around the world to mark various anniversaries, the most recent being their 30th anniversary in 2024.

The pop trio found a new band of fans in Vietnam in 2023 after recording a version of their hit *I Do* with Vietnamese artist Duc Phuc. This song is now their second most popular on Spotify, and they have experienced a second wave of fame at the other side of the globe. ▶▶

Lee, centre, alongside the other 911 members in the 90s

A big star in his own right!

BRIAN LITTRELL

While the Backstreet Boys are still gigging (mostly in Las Vegas), several of the band members also have their own careers outside of this. Alongside Backstreet Boys gigs, vocalist Brian Littrell launched a solo music career focusing on contemporary Christian music in the early 2000s, which has proved popular in America. He is also a big supporter of his son, Baylee Littrell, who was on *American Idol* in 2025 and now has a successful career as a country singer.

Having suffered from congenital issues throughout his life, Littrell started a charity, the Health Hearty Club for Kids, in the late 90s. This provided education, rehabilitation and motivation for children with congenital heart defects. While the charity is no longer active, Brian continues to offer support for those suffering from heart defects today through the American Heart Association.

Brian, second left, with the Boys in 1997!

KEITH DUFFY

Boyzone vocalist Keith Duffy has carried on a career in entertainment, moving into acting. He is perhaps best-known for his stint as a soap star. When Boyzone members initially broke up to pursue solo projects in 1999, Keith soon became known for his appearances as heartthrob barman Ciaran McCarthy on *Coronation Street*. Duffy spent nine years on the show but later said that the role prevented him from branching out in his acting career, as he was forever typecast thanks to this job. He did appear in other TV series though, including Irish soap *Fair City*, children's series *Little Roy* and reality series *The Door*.

Duffy has also appeared in various stage shows including Billy Roche's *A Handful of Stars, Dandelions* and *Big Maggie*. The eagle-eyed will have spotted him in the role of a security guard in 2014's *Mrs Brown's Boys D'Movie*. Duffy has also spent much of his time raising funds for autism charities after his daughter was diagnosed with the condition at 18 months old. In 2016 Duffy came together with Westlife's Brian McFadden to create supergroup Boyzlife, which is still active today. The duo perform both Boyzone and Westlife hits at popular live shows around the world.

We loved Keith in *Corrie*!

Keith, centre, with Boyzone in 1993

With Brian McFadden as Boyzlife!

ULTIMATE QUIZ!

We test how closely you've been paying attention to our boyband trivia!

1 What was Take That's original band name, chosen by the initial incarnation of Gary Barlow and Mark Owen?

2 Many consider East 17's *Stay Another Day* to be a Christmas song, but what is the song about?

3 Which NSYNC member had originally auditioned to be a member of the Backstreet Boys?

4 What year did Justin Timberlake release his first solo album?

5 What was Five's first major international hit?

6 Which confectionery company released limited edition chocolate bars featuring members of Westlife in 2001?

7 What year did Brian McFadden leave Westlife?

116

8 What did Ronan Keating do for work before his music career?

9 How many Take That singles made it to number one in the UK?

10 What age was Nick Carter when he joined the Backstreet Boys?

11 Who was in the original line-up of the Backstreet Boys?

12 Who originally wrote and released *Uptown Girl*, which was later covered by Westlife?

13 Which talent manager created Boyzone?

14 Which Take That back-up dancer did Gary Barlow marry?

117

15 Who was the founding member of East 17?

16 How did the members of Boyz II Men meet?

17 Which 90s boyband have recently had success in Vietnam with a version of their hit, *I Do*, recorded with local artist Duc Phuc?

18 What is NSYNC an acronym for?

19 What was Boyzone's debut album?

21 Which much-loved 90s boyband opened the 2000 Brit awards with Queen?

20 How many Grammy awards have Boyz II Men won?

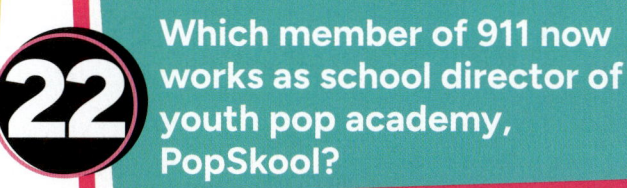

22 Which member of 911 now works as school director of youth pop academy, PopSkool?

23 Which 90s group is considered the most popular boyband in history, based on their record international album sales?

24 Which hit by NYSYNC was featured in the 2024 Marvel film *Deadpool*, sparking a fresh wave of popularity for the song?

25 Which UK artist has taken home the most ever Brit awards, as of 2025?

26 Which of Ronan Keating's children appeared on *The Voice* in 2019?

27 Which controversial 1991 Take That music video was banned from daytime television?

28 Which BBC children's carol competition saw Gary Barlow get his start in music in 1986?

29 Which Backstreet Boys music video was filmed at Los Angelos International Airport?

30 Which 90s boyband released the much-loved hit, *Keep on Movin'*, in 1999?

ANSWERS: 1. The Cutest Rush 2. It was written as a tribute to Tony Mortimer's brother, who had passed away 3. Chris Kirkpatrick 4. 2002 5. When The Lights Go Out 6. 2004 7. Cadbury 8. He worked in a shoe shop in Dublin 9. 12 10. 13 years old 11. A.J. McLean, Howie Dorough, Nick Carter, Kevin Richardson and Brian Littrell 12. Billy Joel 13. Louis Walsh 14. Dawn Andrews 15. Tony Mortimer, who approached London Records in 1991 16. At Philadelphia High School for the Performing Arts 17. 911 18. The band name used the last letter of each member's name: Justin, Chris, Joey, Jason and JC 19. Said and Done 20. Four 21. Five 22. Spike Dawbarn 23. The Backstreet Boys, who have sold over 100 million records worldwide 24. Bye Bye Bye 25. Robbie Williams, who has won 13 26. Missy Keating 27. Do What U Like 28. Song for Christmas 29. I Want it That Way 30. Five

119

Behind the Hits!

We look back at the truly iconic teen pop magazine *Smash Hits*

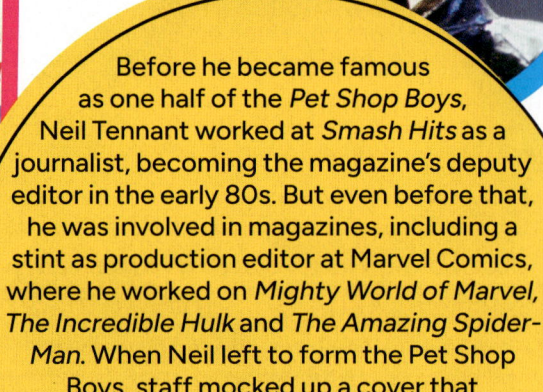

Before he became famous as one half of the *Pet Shop Boys*, Neil Tennant worked at *Smash Hits* as a journalist, becoming the magazine's deputy editor in the early 80s. But even before that, he was involved in magazines, including a stint as production editor at Marvel Comics, where he worked on *Mighty World of Marvel*, *The Incredible Hulk* and *The Amazing Spider-Man*. When Neil left to form the Pet Shop Boys, staff mocked up a cover that proclaimed: "How I left Britain's greatest pop magazine to become a pop star and then came back with my tail between my legs." Which, of course, he never did…

One of *Smash Hits'* many USPs was its forensic printing of song lyrics – which wasn't an easy feat in the days before this was officially done by record companies. Headphone-wearing staff would hunch over the office record player where they played a single over and over again, while scribbling down the lyrics. Every "ooh", "ah" and "sigh" had to be included or there would be a backlash from fans.

Westlife perform at the *Smash Hits* Poll Winners Party

In the late 1980s, the mag's publisher EMAP tried to replicate *Smash Hits* in the United States. Sadly, it didn't take off, partly because American pop fans didn't fully 'get' the title's very British humour. More successful was the annual TV awards show, the *Smash Hits* Poll Winners Party, which ran from 1988 to 2005.

The magazine's general ethos was that pop stars were fab, but also slightly absurd. So as well as having daft questions fired at them, the magazine team also gave celebs ridiculous names. So Adam Ant was called "Alan Ant", Paul McCartney "Fab Macca Wacky Thumbs Aloft", Chris de Burgh (generally considered a bit dull by the magazine) became Chris de Bleeurgh. Dave Hepworth, one of *Smash Hits*' early editors, came up with the idea of calling Spandau Ballet's lead singer Tony "Foghorn" Hadley and depicted the Human League's Phil Oakey as living in a house where his father and the budgie had the same lopsided hair.

The magazine always tried to stay cheeky and irreverent. Questions would often be completely left-field, like: If you were a kitchen appliance, what would you be? Does your mother play golf? Or what's the worst song you've ever written? (once asked of George Michael who replied *Bad Boys*) Some pop stars embraced the anarchy, while others didn't get the joke and would sometimes flounce out of interviews – all of which would then be reported gleefully in print.

At its height, the fortnightly magazine sold over one million copies each issue, making it one of the best-selling magazines of all time. It became so influential amongst teenagers that even politicians wanted in. Prime Minister Margaret Thatcher was given the full *Smash Hits* treatment in 1987, and was cleverly rinsed by the magazine's infamous writer Tom Hibbert.

BACKSTREET BOYS

MEET THE BOYBAND HIT-MAKER

Songwriter John McLaughlin penned much of our 90s soundtrack – and he's still very much going strong!

John McLaughlin

He's been dubbed "the one man hit factory" for writing our soundtrack of the 90s. The main aim of songwriter John McLaughlin was to pen the songs that touched teenage girls' hearts.

From writing hits like *Bodyshakin'* and *All I Want Is You* for 911 to penning his first number one, *Queen Of My Heart* for Westlife, hit-maker John recalls the era that changed his life – and his fortune.

Speaking just weeks after staging a successful tribute show to the late great Shane McGowan, John – who is still a leading light in the music industry – admits he owes his current success to the 90s.

"It's funny how I ended up doing this, as I started off in punk rock bands. I was in my first band at 13.

"It wasn't getting me very far, but I continued to be in bands and write songs."

Then while recovering from a life-threatening illness, John had a lightbulb moment.

He explains, "I had a really bad bout of pneumonia, was in and out of hospital a lot, and while recovering, I was watching a lot of daytime TV. Take That were just starting out.

"I started to look into that – and I started having a go at writing some of these kinda songs.

"As serendipity would have it, I bumped into a guy called Steve Gilmour who put 911 together. We became friends and he asked me to write some songs.

"I met the boys and I could see how athletic and acrobatic they were when dancing to cover versions.

"So, in the first week of writing my pop songs, we wrote *Bodyshakin'*, a song they could have a dance to, *Don't Make Me Wait*, *Love Sensation* and *The Journey*.

"We wrote about five of their big hits, so that was a good start. It was a great learning curve to start off with 911."

Hot on the heels of Take That, bands like Boyzone, Bad Boys Inc, and East 17 broke through. But none of them were from Scotland, that's where 911 were different (despite being named after the American emergency phone number).

And John was involved from the very beginning, sending faxes and calling record companies from his council office job!

"It was on a shoestring. It was on a DIY label with no budget. And I quickly realised, when I got my accidental job in the education department, I could use this as my office. Steve Gilmour was delighted!" he laughed.

"Our aim was always to try and make successful records – to get in the charts and show people what we can do – without a major record company at first. We

> **Our aim was always to try and make successful records – to get in the charts and show people what we can do – without a major record company**

concentrated on writing the best songs we could in order to do that, without any financial backing," explained John, who turned 60 in January.

"I will tell you a wee story: I wrote *When The Lights Go Out* with Elliot Kennedy. It was actually for 911, for their second album, but the boss of Virgin Records didn't particularly like it. But I played it to Simon Cowell and he loved it and took it for Five. That's the power of songs.

"Simon told me, 'This song is going to be a big hit in America', and he was totally right."

John went on to win the BMI Award in America for one million airplays of *When The Lights Go Out*.

That was a career highlight. So was receiving a

John worked closely with 911

A number one success for Westlife!

With legendary Motown songwriter Lamont Dozier

Friends with the late, great Shane McGowan

Tartan Clef Living Legend Award in 2013, and achieving his first number one, when Westlife's *Queen Of My Heart* topped the charts in 2001 to gain their ninth number one.

"I remember it and it was incredible – what a feeling. We did *Top Of The Pops* and everything. We also had a few number twos for *Bodyshakin'*, *All I Want Is You* and *When The Lights Go Out* was number three here."

John, who is from Milton in Glasgow, is the eldest of seven children.

He had a happy upbringing, surrounded by music "from Neil Diamond to Motown to Frank Sinatra", but "never had any money". Until the 1990s, when his fortune changed for the better.

"Music was really important to us. ▶▶

With another boyband legend, Take That's Mark Owen!

Another famous pal – Rod Stewart!

Performing in a Shane McGowan tribute show

So, for me to go on and have success in it, it's just been amazing.

"It was incredible because the success changed everything. I could help my family a lot more. I was completely driven by it."

To this day, John continues to work in the music industry. In tribute to his pal and lead singer of The Pogues, Shane McGowan, John wrote the musical *For The Love Of Shane McGowan* which has become a huge success.

"I worked with Shane for years and it's grown arms and legs.

"We just had a sell-out tour and are then taking it around Europe and back to the Edinburgh Fringe."

He is also in the Bay City Rollers and counts Sir Rod Stewart as a good pal!

"And I wake up every day and I am so thankful that this is still what I do.

"Once I got on the bus, I thought, 'I'm not getting off'.

"I got to work with all my heroes: Rod Stewart, Shane McGowan, Echo And The Bunnymen and Simon Cowell, all because of pop music. It opened so many doors. It's been incredible and I love it with as much vigour as I did then."

With his thirty-plus-years music career behind him, at 60, John has never been busier. And even when he is not writing for artists, performing with The Bay City Rollers or with his own band Johnny Mac And The Faithful, he's still making money, thanks to the recent 90s boyband revival and royalties.

"I am over the moon when I see all these reunion tours, because it means I am getting paid all over again! Every time a song is played on the radio, you get radio royalties, and you get record sale royalties from all the digital and physical sales. And then you get a percentage of the door money from these shows. This is why whenever we see a boyband doing a 42-date tour, that's happy days for me!

"When you are a songwriter, as long as your band has some kind of success or comeback, it's a constant income. It's a blessing for the work you put in to get those songs going. I have been very, very lucky."

In a full-circle moment, John was recently reunited with Lee, Spike and Jimmy of 911 when the Bay City Rollers were on the same line-up at a festival – some 30 years after they first boarded the boyband bus!

> "I got to work with all my heroes: Rod Stewart, Shane McGowan, Echo And The Bunnymen and Simon Cowell, all because of pop music. It opened so many doors. It's been incredible and I love it with as much vigour as I did then"

John now tours with the Bay City Rollers

John says, "There were great writers at that time like Steve Mac and Wayne Hector and a lot of Swedish writers were amazing. The song I wish I'd written? *Flying Without Wings* was a beautifully written song and so was *I Want It That Way*. Very simple songs with great lyrics and melodies."

SONGS JOHN WROTE…

HIS PERSONAL FAVOURITE:

QUEEN OF MY HEART FOR WESTLIFE
CHARTED AT NO. 1
"It's my favourite song I have written because it is so Celtic, and that's what Simon wanted. And because it was number one is pretty special. I like how that record sounds."

TOP HITS:

PARTY PEOPLE FRIEND NIGHT FOR 911
CHARTED AT NO. 5

ALL I WANT IS YOU FOR 911
CHARTED AT NO. 4

THE JOURNEY FOR 911
CHARTED AT NO. 3

I WISH I WAS A PUNK ROCKER FOR SANDY THOM
CHARTED AT NO. 1

WHAT I GO TO SCHOOL FOR FOR BUSTED
CHARTED AT NO. 3

YOU SAID NO FOR BUSTED
CHARTED AT NO. 1

WHEN THE LIGHTS GO OUT FOR FIVE
CHARTED AT NO. 4